Sex: A Manual for Better Sex

Helpful Health Hints and Tips

Volume 3

What's Your Fetish?

CONTENTS

Introduction

Have you ever felt like your love life was a non-starter? Perhaps you had a great love life in the past but it began to seem mundane. There is so much help out there these days that you really can get your love life back on track with very little effort. Win her heart all over again or win his! This book is a practical manual that is loaded with information that you may not have known. Do you know what women see as sexy? What about your man? The problems happen because there is a very wide gap between the way that women see sex and the way that men do. However, once you understand those differences you can exploit them to give you the best sex ever.

In attempting to break the barriers in a relationship that can stem from an unhappy or unsatisfied sex life, this book goes over some important practices that can be attempted and tried by people from all walks of life. The book talks about not only how to please each other in the bedroom, but how to please one another outside of bedroom to reflect into the bedroom. This book talks about why these actions are important and how they can affect your sexual relationship when they are done correctly and when they are not done at all. Sex is one of the most intimate parts about being in a relationship, having a sex life that is less than ideal can cause a relationship to crumble.

This book also goes over the importance of communication in a relationship. How one can believe they are communicating with the other when they really aren't. I will guide you through the different myths and stereotypes following different types of practices and show you the importance of opening up your wild side in the bedroom.

Did you also know that your health matters as far as great sex is concerned? We will give you great tips and tricks that you can employ to make your sex life better at any age at all. The way that you approach sex and the way that you treat your body have a lot in common and the care that you put into both activities should be equally caring. We will show you how to care for your body in such a way as to make yourself alluring and also switch that ignition light back on again.

Sometimes it is the mundanity of being with one partner over an extended period of time that can seem to kill off your love life, but in actual fact, it isn't a change in chemicals or anything that is logical. It's a change of point of view. Keep the passion alive by actually sharing that passion because once you do, you will find that you can discuss anything with your partner and expect them to respond.

While many believe sex is simply done with two individuals and nothing else, this book shows you how to spice up a fizzled sex life by the use of different types of sex toys, edibles, anal sex and oral sex. Finding the line between taboo and social norms can be difficult for some individuals. If you feel as though you are categorized as someone who delves into taboo like practices, you will be surprised to know that everyone around the world, culturally, views sex differently than others. You cannot expect cultures that are hundreds of years old to practice social norms in the modern society because as far as the culture is concerned, the time period in regards to sex has not changed.

There is an interesting difference between the way that guys views sex and the way that girls do. We take a look at what turns a man on and what turns a girl on because without knowing those secrets, you may just be pressing the wrong buttons. This book is a handy guide for couples just starting out, for those who have been married for a long time and for those a little nervous about their ability in bed. Believe me, you are not alone. So many people worry about not being able to perform and performance anxiety may be getting in the way. We explain how to move forward from this and get everything working like it was intended to.

Chapter 1 –
What Girls Want in Bed

I started with this because most men actually want to know if they are doing things in the right way and will be concerned about whether their girl is seeing things in the same way as they are. Men are the protectors. They are the ones who are the hunters, and when it comes to sex, many don't have a clue because in their role as provider, they haven't taken the time to find out what women like. We asked over 100 women about their likes and dislikes in the bedroom and this may help you and may also show you what your woman probably wants. When women talk together, they are open and frank about things such as their sex life, though because of their emotional and caring nature and unlikely to criticize their man or try to explain what they are doing wrong because, quite frankly, they don't want to upset him or challenge his masculinity. Thus, unsatisfactory bedroom situations are quite normal without this communication. I am hoping that the answers I got from guys and from girls will help you all to stop fighting each other by refusing to talk about your needs. Communicating your needs in the bedroom is the only way to assure that you will be pleasured the way you desire. The top things that girls said that were missing in their bedroom experience were these:

Number One complaint was that women do not climax enough. Because a man's climax is obvious, he can't get away with faking it. However, the majority of women who were interviewed had faked orgasm several times in order to make their men feel better about sex, but had not actually experienced orgasm while making love. Girls want to come as much as men do, but since men have trouble understanding the female anatomy, it's little wonder that they don't know how to make a woman climax. I think if you are arguing this point, then you need to watch <u>this video</u>. It's actually hilarious and shows how little men know about the delicate parts of a woman. If a man is not aware of the anatomy of a woman, how is he supposed to find all of those places that give her orgasm? We will cover this later in the book.

Inability to climax is a common problem among women. However, it is not always attributed to the male's lack of knowledge on the female anatomy. Many factors take place in determining if a woman will be able to climax. Men are much more visual; women are more emotional. Simply stimulating woman with foreplay does not always lead to her ability to climax because woman need much more "warming up" than men do. It can be hard for a woman to climax if she isn't in the mood for sex, making it even more difficult for both parties. Woman know that in a lot of cases, the inability to climax can be related to factors outside of what is going on in the bedroom; work stress, home stress, relationship issues, biological or genetic predisposition, etc. Knowing the female anatomy can certainly give you an advantage when exploring the realms of your woman, so be sure the study up or watch the video. Being unable to find the clitoris and not knowing what the cervix feels like with your finger can be a huge turn off for woman. Women want to think you are experienced, even if you know you are not.

Number two complaint was sweat. Women really don't like it. Although it's part of the masculine image, women would prefer that the only sweat that happens in bed is that which is generated together during sex. Men who smell turn them off. Feet are among the odors that women hate and which certainly turn them off. Although in times of exhaustive intercourse, it can be hard to prevent sweat from accumulating and dripping onto the other person. If you love the other person, this issue should be trivial. However, because some people are squeamish about bodily fluids in general, it would be advised to keep a cloth or a hand towel nearby to wipe down areas of the body that are most prone to sweating. For some people, it's the hands and feet, for others, it's the face, neck, and shoulders.

A lot of the smell associated with sweat is bacteria. Sweat, when first presenting itself, normally has a nonexistent to mild odor. Once the sweat has sat in a damp, concealed space such as the feet, armpits, and in other crevices near and around your genitals, the bacteria that begin to grow and accumulate are the reason for the pungent odor. Keeping yourself clean can help to prevent these odors.

Scrubbing your feet and placing them back into the same bacteria ridden, smelly shoes is basically eliminating all of your hygienic efforts because the bacteria is just going to re accumulate on your feet while wearing the shoes. Clean your shoes, if you can, with the washing machine, sink or a hose. Any areas of your body that are prone to sweat throughout the day, those are the areas that you should focus and clean the most when you are taking a shower, to avoid bacteria build up.

Number three complaint was that men have little imagination when it comes to positions. In many of the relationships of women interviewed, they came to the same conclusion. During the first flashes of passion, yes – men are quite imaginative, but then they revert to this boring style where missionary position is the only option. Come on boys, girls want more than that. Lack of imagination can stem from lack of experience as well. Many women don't feel comfortable taking the lead in the bedroom because they believe that is the man's job. If the man has not had a whole lot of experience with a variety of positions, he will probably just stick to what he knows. As the relationship grows and you become more comfortable with one another, new positions should be introduced.

When the introduction of new positions fails to happen, this is where the frustration sets in.

Some men are not comfortable expressing their sexuality out of fear they will be rejected. Many times, they figure out what they believe the woman to enjoy and stick to that. After years and years of the same position, it can begin to become mundane and routine doing the same positions over and over again, leading to problems in and out of the bedroom. By communicating with one another about what positions to try next, couples can avoid becoming stagnant and can help boost the man's confidence to be adventurous and try new things.

Although imagination can be a good thing in the bedroom, when one is not used to it, it can come as a surprise to the other. When introducing different types of sexual techniques and practices, be sure that the other is on the same page and is willing to humor the request. You would hate to be rejected while in the middle of a sex session.

Number four complaint although this complaint was across the board and was one of the most annoying – is that men turn over and go to sleep directly after sex and do not see that women need to be hugged. Although sex is a physical thing and you may be tired, women are not animals. They want more than a hump. They want a hump with all the trimmings. Thus, hugs are an essential part of that. This means before, during and after. It's reassuring and makes a woman feel safe and loved.

More often than not, women are wide awake after sex, unlike the man. Having the man turn over and put his back to you after sex can feel as though he "got what he wanted, now he is done with you". No woman wants to feel this way. Cuddling and snuggling after sex can be one of the most intimate parts of being together, don't ignore such a simple action. Even so much as kissing and hugging afterwards and telling her how much you care about her can be all the reassurance and attention she needs. Women cannot expect men to know that this bothers them unless they voice their concerns. Sex is meant to be both emotional and physical, not cuddling and hugging throughout the act can take all the emotions out of it and make it feel cold and shallow. Number five complaint was that often a man was not that interested in foreplay. As long as he was getting what he wanted, he didn't seem to care too much if this was causing discomfort to his woman. This was particularly relevant in the older range of women that I interviewed and the conclusion was that more foreplay was needed to help with lubrication. Often men blamed lack of lubrication on the woman when in fact it was the lack for foreplay that made the situation worse than it would have been. Play fair boys because you get better sex out of it and so does she.

Foreplay is one of the most important parts of sex. Passion and intimacy are at its highest points during foreplay. This is a time when you show the woman how much you love her and her body and how much it excites you. Without foreplay, you are not only going to make sex less than desirable for her, you are not going to have as nearly as much enjoyment as you would if you had stimulated her prior to penetration.

Woman take a lot longer to warm up for sex than men, although it is seemingly common for men to receive foreplay before sex without reciprocation. So, not only does the man get an immediate erection, he also gets the pleasure of receiving oral sex as "warming up". Women need to be warmed up to provide proper lubrication and comfort when being penetrated. When the vagina and the clitoris are stimulated, they naturally puff up and secrete fluids, making penetration easier and more enjoyable for both parties involved. Not only does foreplay allow the women and men to engage in intercourse comfortably, but it also allows the woman a better chance for climaxing during penetration, which is a difficult task for many women. Statistics show that women are more prone to climax without penetration. One would argue that the reason women have such a difficult time climaxing is because of the general and widespread lack of enthusiastic foreplay among the population of men.

You can see from these complaints that there is a world of difference between the way that women view sex and the way that men do. We shall devote a chapter and let men have their say within that chapter, though it is important to note, there were other complaints from women that pointed to the following turn-offs. If you are guilty of any of these, then it will help your love life if you do something to attempt to correct the situation:

- Women don't like bad odor
- Bad breath is a turn off
- Women don't like guys in baggy pants – they want to see your behind
- White pants and plaid shorts are out!
- Track suits are a turn off and a sign that a man is too lazy to actually have a waistband
- Tee shirts that are too short and show off a pot belly

From this you can summarize that women like men who look after themselves and who really do present themselves in a sexy, clean and fresh way. Generally speaking, if a man does not present himself in a way that shows he takes good care of himself, this has a potential to be a reflection of the way he will treat his woman. Although that is not always the case, first impressions can be critical when meeting a new person and you always want to look as though you care, if even for a moment. The man should also be aware of his woman's needs and be prepared to give as well as to take. Giving means giving more than the inches you were born with. It means giving from the heart and being aware of your woman's emotions.

Chivalry is not dead and with the rising generation of younger, more independent woman, men may feel intimidated when offering help or going out of their way to hold the door or pull out a chair. When it comes to relationships and dating, simple, chivalrous gestures generally aren't going to scare away women, they are going to show them that you care enough to make them comfortable. Take care of yourself and don't overlook the simple gestures that can make all the difference in how woman see or perceive you.

Chapter 2 –

What Men Want in Bed

If you are a girl and have a smug look on your face following the last chapter, don't be too quick to think that girls got off lightly. There are so many things that turn men on and off and you, too, need to be aware of them. Talking to 100 men, to try and keep things well balanced, what we found was that the answers were pretty universal.

Men like nudity – Although you may think that sexy nighty is wonderful, men prefer to see you in the nude and will do all they can to remove it as quickly as possible. Although this is the general "purpose" of lingerie, some men find it a nuisance and prefer to have you prance around the house in it as opposed to wearing it during sexual intercourse. If you really want to turn your man on, save your money. Use the money you save on making your body look as good as it can and you will win the day. Spend that money to keep up your skin and hair and basic hygienic needs. Similar to how a man cares for himself by showering, buying clothing, buying cologne, etc. Women are also expected to provide general care for themselves for the same reasons. People want to know that the person they are interested in can and will take care of themselves.

Men like the lights on. They want to appreciate their woman. If you are one of those women who turn the lights off the moment you get under the covers, stop and think about it. It's a great compliment that your man wants to see you naked and even if you think you are not the best built package on the block, he is with you. He will be more turned on by seeing you naked than feeling you cower away from the light in shame.

Being able to see you during intercourse arouses the man. Men are more visual, as stated previously, meaning that being able to see how they are pleasuring their significant other can arouse them tremendously. As a woman, being ashamed of imperfections is foolish because the man you are with should love you and all of your imperfections. No one is perfect, that is what makes you perfect for him. Embrace your imperfections as your own unique identity and have sex with the lights on.

Men do like sexy underwear. A woman who wears sexy underwear is thought of as much more aware of her man's needs and wants and also very much in touch with her own femininity. If you have taken to wearing old fashioned cotton, swap it because although it may feel good, it isn't for the bedroom. Picking out underwear for your woman can also be a good alternative if your woman tends to buy underwear that is less than attractive. Instead of telling her directly that her choice in underwear is less than desirable, buy her a pair that you find attractive and say you want her to wear them before you both engage in sexual intercourse the next time. This can be a good hint for her without a direct insult.

On the side of women, wearing cute and attractive underwear during the day can help boost your confidence by knowing you look sexy underneath your outfit. Having a man compliment you on your choice of underwear is flattering and helps boost self-esteem. Plus, cotton can cut off airflow to the vagina, causing a potential for irritation and infection should anything happen.

Men are turned on by women who are not afraid to become a vamp in bed. Of course, they don't want a woman who is cheap in her presentation to others. This is just for the bedroom. However, even the primmest of women can appear very sexy in the bedroom and the man knows it's just for him. That makes it even more of a turn on.

Women who know when and how to take control can be a huge turn on. Sex is exhausting and as a man, a huge portion of sex is left as his responsibility. Knowing that the woman he is with will let him sit back while she takes the reins can be comforting and exciting. It also helps to spice up redundant sex if the man is always the one initiating. Have the woman initiate for a change. Routine in the bedroom should always be avoided.

Some guys are turned on by women who are career minded and know what they want. They see them as a challenge and for those highly intelligent guys, this presents a great opportunity in bed. Challenging women are not scared to let her man know what she wants and that's powerful stuff under the sheets.

A woman with goals and ambitions says a lot about her character and can also be a good reflection of her attitude in the bedroom. If she likes to be in control of her future, she may be the same way in the bedroom. Certain goals and aspirations can parallel sexual desire, so pay attention. Men tend to gravitate towards women that are more of a challenge to obtain because the reward is greater overall. Anyone and everyone can get the easy girl, but men really want the girl that is hard to get. This has been the case since the beginning of time, throughout our entire childhoods. The woman who is the easiest to get, will be shared around with everyone. The woman who is hard to get, will be enjoyed by only a select few. This is the difference between diamonds and dirt. Dirt is abundant and can be obtained by anyone. Diamonds are expensive and are only obtained through hard work, wealth and patience.

Men adore women who are happy within the skin they are in. They don't want to babysit insecurity. The problem with women who are insecure is that they are too needy and demand too much emotional stuff and that's not a male thing – that is unless the male is particularly domineering in all the wrong ways. Needy women generally get lumbered with men who want to own them and relationships such as this are not the best in bed. If you want happy sex – learn to love yourself because if you show signs of insecurity, it's a real turn off for a man.

They always say that in order to love someone else you have to love yourself first. This is incredibly true. Whenever someone feels as though they are inadequate or less than desirable to their significant other, this causes strain and tension on the relationship. A woman who is confident in her appearance and herself is going to do a myriad better in a relationship than a woman who does not love herself. Emotional insecurities weigh down a relationship as well, so finding confidence in not only your appearance, but in yourself and your self-worth is important.

Too much makeup is a turn off for men. They prefer to see a woman for who she is, not who she would like to be. Be yourself. Let your wildness out and he will thank you for it. However, be aware that there's a certain amount of wildness that isn't acceptable. For example, body hair will be a real turn off for him. Instead of spending loads on makeup to cover up who you are, spend it on things that soften your skin and give it a sexy glow and make sure that you wax regularly.

When we say wildness we generally mean attitude related, not physically related (unless the couple is into that). Men prefer woman who portray the "lady in the street but a freak in the bed," persona. Classy and put together in appearance but like a wild animal between the sheets. Many women tend to hide this side of themselves for fear of rejection. Never sell yourself short and settle for less than what you desire because you are afraid you will not be accepted. The pet hates of men are shown below because these are real turn offs as far as the male of the species is concerned:

- Don't keep asking "Do you love me?" – You should already know.
- Don't smell of sweat – always shower before bed
- Don't talk about your periods
- Don't cut your toenails in front of him
- Girls who try to dress cute at home – it doesn't work. Be yourself.

Basically men like to know what they are getting. It doesn't turn them on to be with someone who isn't happy with themselves or someone who tries to be something that she is not. A self-assured woman who is consistent and who is comfortable with her emotions and body is far more of a turn on than one who is trying to play the part of a whore, and failing badly.

In fact, the use of bad language in bed may even be enough to make him turn over and go to sleep. He wants you as you are rather than how you think you should be. Stop playing games. Get down and dirty, but do it honestly. If you are going to introduce dirty talk, let it be something you are both privy to and are willing to try together. Otherwise you are likely to fall flat on your face because some people do not favor dirty talk.

If you would like to introduce dirty talk, casually mention it in conversation to see if it may be something she is interested in. If she is not one to talk about sexual relations outside of the bedroom, simply start off by talking dirty in short, neutral sayings. Refrain from the use of slang terms like "slut, whore, and bitch" until you know for sure it is something she will be comfortable hearing during intercourse. Using profanity lightly in the bedroom can be a huge turn on for some, and a turn off for others so make sure you prepare accordingly.

It is a well-known stereotype that a man will settle for any woman or sexual partner he can get because he "has a penis" or he "thinks between his legs". This is not always the case. Not all men are open to everything and not all women are open to everything, meaning each person is different and has different desires. Men are historically known for being more instinctually driven when it comes to sex and the bedroom because they have always been looked too as the providers for the family. Men and women alike won't always want to sleep with whomever they can get into the bedroom. Most people are looking for long-term relationships.

Chapter 3 –

The Art of Foreplay

No great sexual experience can ever be complete without foreplay. Foreplay is a crucial part of the sexual act and without it, sex can become mundane and not that exciting. This is why mastering the art of foreplay is what makes the difference between great lovers and the mediocre ones.

While foreplay may seem like something fun people enjoy doing, it is actually necessary for the human sexual experience. Without foreplay, it is extremely difficult to achieve the required levels of sexual excitement and eventually reach orgasm.

Foreplay allows the partners to get physically and mentally ready for the sexual act itself. While performing various foreplay actions, you and your partner will become aroused; hormones will be secreted, and your genitals will get ready for what is to come. If, however, you avoid foreplay the woman may not be ready for the sexual act, which may end up being painful and not satisfying.

While people always assume that foreplay entails only "making out" before sex, there are actually many parts of the human experience that may be considered foreplay. Anything from looks to touches, from text messages to verbal allusions, and light petting to oral sex may be considered foreplay. True foreplay masters start foreplay hours, if not days before the act itself, building up sexual tension to be released through powerful orgasms.

In essence, you may split foreplay into two basic categories. The first category includes everything that happens outside of the bedroom or away from the actual sexual intercourse. The other category involves the actual physical foreplay that goes on just before sex. Here are some basic tips to keep in mind while considering both of these categories.

Foreplay Outside Of the Bedroom

When you want to have sex with someone, you will know it without a doubt. If the person is interested in you as well, or if you are dating or married and having regular sexual relations, you will want to build up some tension and prepare your partner for the sexual experience long before it is actually happening.

This may be achieved through a number of ways, all leading up to the act to come. You will want to spark their imagination to the point where they are thinking about having sex with you, even in those moments when they should not be thinking about it. This way, they will be more than ready when the moment finally arrives, and if you are lucky, they will even initiate it themselves, making things even hotter.

Talk about sex: I don't just mean going on and on about random sexual things. Rather, try to use subtle language to let her or him know you want them. The deeper your relationship, the more freedom you will have. For instance, you will not want to tell a girl you just met what kind of things that you would like to do to her right then and there, while your girlfriend may love you whispering in her ear in a crowded room about your deepest dirty fantasy.

Sexual conversations will certainly get your partner thinking about sex, and if there is sexual chemistry between you, it is likely to get them to think about sex with you. This always points in your favor as the more they think about it, the more ready they will be when the moment finally comes.

Text Her: Are you married and working late? No problem. Text your lady from the office and let her know you are missing her and can't wait to have her in your arms. It will get her imagination going and you may be in for a surprise when you get home.

Same goes for the ladies. There is nothing a man likes more than to know his girl wants him, so let him know. If you are at a point in your relationship where sex is a normal topic, don't be embarrassed to let him know when you are thinking about him sexually. The next time you see him, you will likely get much better sexual treatment.

Buy Sexual Gifts: There is nothing wrong with getting your lady some sexy lingerie or gifts of an even more sexual nature. This will both make her think about you in a sexual way and make her feel wanted. Send her lingerie to her home address with a note like, "Can't wait to see you in it." This will get things heated up long before you reach the bedroom and it is likely you will get a very nice treat out of it.

Foreplay in the Bedroom

Once the sexual act is near, the real hands-on foreplay begins. Hopefully by this time you have built up some sexual tension through the various techniques discussed previously, and now is the time to get the action started.

When it comes to sex, taking things slowly is usually the best way to go. While there may be some exceptions, in most cases you will want things to last as long as possible and to experience as much sexual pleasure as you can. This is why gentle and slow foreplay should precede sex to get both partners ready for the actual act.

Ease into It: In most cases, you will want to ease into sex. You want to slowly explore each other's bodies and get to know each other physically. Simply jumping into action and leaping to penetration will be less pleasing and often painful for the woman. Instead, make her feel special and wanted. Her body will thank you for it, and the actual sexual act will be easier and a lot more satisfying to both partners.

Instead of jumping right into action, kiss each other's bodies, explore each other with your hands and touch every part before going all the way. Don't be afraid to try different things to find out what your partner enjoys. The longer the foreplay, the more intensive the sexual act.

Listen To Your Partner: When I say listen, I don't just mean the words they say. Listen to their body language as well, and try to understand what they like and don't like. There is no shame in asking your partner verbally if they like something either, but there is a lot to be gathered from the way their body reacts to certain things as well.

For instance, most women enjoy being kissed on the neck, but some might not. Feel free to give it a shot, but if you see she is unresponsive don't push it, as it may end up being annoying for her.

If body language is not enough, open a dialogue. Ask your partner if there is something, in particular, they enjoy or dislike. After all, you are adults and likely not to be each other's first partner, so why not use the experience you both already have and make your sex life better. Sex is a perfectly natural and normal thing, and there is nothing to be ashamed of in the bedroom.

Explore Her Body: Use your hands, your fingers and your lips to explore each other's bodies. Some people have restrictions about what they want to do in bed, but you should really feel comfortable touching and kissing your partner just about anywhere if you are going to have sex.

Sexual experiences should be free and liberating, not restricting, especially if you know what your partner likes you should feel free to pursue it. If not, explore and find out with both your fingers and your tongue. Kissing each other's bodies is an erotic way of showing that you are really into it and not just trying to get it over with.

Undress Each Other: While it is fine to remove your own clothes before or during foreplay, letting your partner do it and doing it for him or her will make things that much more exciting. Take off one piece of clothing at a time and continue to kiss and touch in-between. This way, the tension will build gradually and things will go smoother.

Talk Dirty: This is one move to be careful with as it can quickly backfire, especially for guys, but when done properly it can be very exciting for both partners. There is nothing wrong with finding out a little about what your partner likes in this sense before you begin, but sometimes it will come down to trying things out, and you will want to tread lightly so as not to offend your partner.

Once you understand what he or she is comfortable with, though, many people will be able to use dirty talk to spark up the action and make things a lot more exciting in bed.

Chapter 4 –
It Doesn't End with the Orgasm

Despite what many of us, usually men would like to believe, sex does not end with the Big-O. Just as foreplay is an important part of sex physically, mentally and emotionally, so too is the after-play. While after-play may have much more to do with the emotional aspect of things than foreplay, it is very important and should not be neglected or forgotten.

After-play is a much simpler thing to master than foreplay. Instead of fancy techniques, what you want to do is show your partner, especially the female, some attention. Women like to feel special and important and simply jumping out of bed once the action is done will not make them feel that way at all. On the contrary, it may very often make them feel dirty and as if they have done something wrong, when the reality is they did not.

After-play is not reserved solely for men to take care of either. A woman also needs to engage with her partner after sexual intercourse to make things special for both partners, and remember, if you don't offer much after sex you can't really expect to receive much either.

Don't Run Away

There are actually scientific reasons for staying in bed after sexual intercourse. The basic reason comes down to how quickly men and women go back to the pre-sex state after the intercourse ends. Men tend to calm down quickly. Their penis shrinks and all other physical factors such as their heartbeat and blood flow all go back to normal within a very short period of time, making a man basically crash after he has an orgasm. This is often followed by a man desperately wanting to rest and often sleep.

A woman, on the other hand, takes a lot longer to get sexually excited but also to shed the excitement. Once a man has experienced an orgasm and is temporarily unable to perform, a woman will need some time to calm down sexually. This is an experience which women like to share with their partner and remaining in bed next to her, caressing her and making her feel safe and desirable will help her feel like the experience was significant for the both of you. Running off to take a shower can make a woman think she is undesirable, as she will be left there wondering what about sex with her made you feel so dirty.

Some men even have the tendency to leave altogether, and unless you want the woman to feel cheap, you should not do this. Even if she tells you it is ok to go as soon as you are done, you should remain there with her for a while. Every woman will appreciate it, even if your connection is not extremely emotional.

Sex often happens in an environment perfect for sleep. You will more often than not be in a comfortable bed at night, in a warm room, next to someone who is special to you. This means your body will want to fall asleep and relax, and this is perfectly fine,

especially following the intense experience of an orgasm. Still, you should make yourself stay up a little while longer on purpose to remain with your partner. After a certain amount of time, especially if it is bed time anyway, you have every right to go to sleep, and you will both probably enjoy sleeping next to each other after a sexual act.

The responsibility can't be put completely on the man as not all men know what women want. Instead, feel free to tell your man that you need him to stay with you, hold you, talk to you, or whatever other need you may desire from him. Don't just expect a man to understand and know your needs, just as you often don't understand his. This is all natural and with most instances in life, communication is the key.

In the end, it is important to emphasize that after-play is actually the first step of foreplay for your next sexual encounter, whenever it may happen. Often, the caressing and kissing after a sexual episode will make both partners want to go again, which is great, but even if not, it will leave both partners feeling very satisfied, and the next sexual encounter is likely to be more intense and more fulfilling in general.

Chapter 5 -
Spicing Things Up

There is nothing wrong with "normal" sex in the missionary position, but there are many things you can do during and before sex to spice things up and make your sexual experiences a lot more fun, versatile and exciting.

There is more than one way of getting pleasure and having fun with your partner. In fact, there are dozens of ways, and in this chapter, we will try to cover some of the more exciting ones and give some insight into some of the things you could be doing to either spice up your current love life or try in the future with your next partner.

Switching Positions

If you are inexperienced at sex, the most natural and common way you will be doing it early on is the good old missionary position. The position is often practiced by the much more experienced couples as well and is one of the staples of sex, but it is certainly not the only way to do it. In fact, there are dozens of positions you could be using and books like Kama Sutra can really open up your imagination. That said, this book is too short to present a full list of positions, but we can mention some of the more exciting ones.

Giving the Lady Some Power

While missionary position puts the man in the position of power being on top, switching positions and letting the woman be on top can be very exhilarating for both partners. There are many advantages of a woman being on top.

For starters, with the woman on top, she will have the ability to control the tempo of the action, and since men can often be pretty bad at this, it may be the best way for her to experience pleasure.

The experience is also very exciting for the man, as he has full sight of the woman's body and can see her in full as she enjoys the act and leads the action. Seeing a woman like this is an extreme turn on for men, and you could say that a woman being on top is the sexiest position of all.

This position, often known as the Cowgirl, allows the man to also caress the woman's body, her breasts and even her clitoris which is now fully within reach, with his fingers, or she can do it herself if she wants to, which can even further stimulate the man. Overall, the Cowgirl is an extremely stimulating position for both partners, and every couple should try it at least occasionally, but I recommend introducing it to your sexual menu as often as possible.

Doing Things From Behind

The famous "Doggy Style" position as it is often referred to, is a position that eliminates the face-to-face contact and some of the more romantic aspects of sex, but can be very stimulating to both partners for various other reasons.

For starters, the man will feel very dominant in this position, and for men, domination is often half the fun. Having the woman in such a submissive position can be a major turn-on for the man, but many women also enjoy being dominated to some degree and sex from behind will also arouse many women.

Also very importantly, this position allows the man to penetrate a woman deeper, which may cause additional pleasure depending on various factors, such as penis size. Another additional advantage of this position is that a man can again stimulate the clitoris by reaching around the woman with his hand, or a woman can stimulate it herself to achieve further satisfaction.

An important thing to be careful with is not to hurt a woman when having sex in the Doggy Style position, as the deep penetration may cause you to hurt some of her inner organs when thrusting, which can be very painful.

While the classical Doggy Style includes a woman being on her knees, other versions of this position include a woman lying on the bed face down or on her side with the man lying on top or next to her and entering her from behind, like he would during the regular Doggy Style.

Oral Presentations

Very often, the first form of sex people encounter in their lives is oral sex. Oral sex can be performed by both men and women, and it includes using your mouth, lips and tongue to stimulate a man's penis or a woman's vagina to sexually satisfy them.

Cunnilingus and Fellatio as oral sex for women and men, respectively, is often a very common practice among most partners, but some men and women avoid the practice for various reasons. Some men, for instance, think the vagina is simply not clean enough or does not smell pleasant enough to go anywhere near it with their mouths, while many women also find inserting a man's penis into their mouth unhygienic, or the idea of semen getting on their tongue or anywhere near their mouth disgusting.

Of course, with so many people performing oral sex without any major problems, we can see that these are mostly myths, and oral sex is neither dirty nor disgusting. It does need to be performed with caution, so that hygiene and your partner's feelings, and any issues they may have, are taken into consideration. For instance, if a woman does not want you to ejaculate near her mouth, you should respect this.

Oral sex is extremely stimulating for most men and women, and the fact your partner is giving you such intimate attention can be a major turn on. It is also a very relaxing form of sex as you don't really need to do anything at all other than enjoy yourself. While oral sex is most commonly practiced as a part of the foreplay, it can also be performed all the way to an orgasm, and skilled lovers will lead their partners to orgasms through oral sex just to give them the pleasure.

Anal Sex

Anal sex among straight couples is one of the most controversial topics. Many women won't even consider it, and many men find the practice unnecessary with the vagina right there. Still, for others, anal sex is a regular part of the sexual experience and one they enjoy very much.

If you and your partner decide to experiment with anal sex, it is very important to be careful. Anal sex can cause various problems, including infections, spreading of STDs and pain to the female partner.

Hygiene is the first and foremost thing to think about when having anal sex. The anus is absolutely packed with germs at all times and wiping or washing it will never eliminate all of the germs present. Of course, you should wash thoroughly if you intend to have anal sex, but using a condom is an absolute must with anal sex.

Furthermore, many STDs are even easier to spread via anal sex, which is yet another reason to use condoms during this practice. Very importantly, if you have anal sex, do not try vaginal sex with the same condom, as the germs from the anus have no place in a woman's vagina and will more often than not cause vaginal infections which can be quite nasty and uncomfortable.

The anus is not intended to be penetrated from the outside either, and no natural lubrication will happen through sexual excitement as it does in the vagina. This means you will need to use artificial lubrication to make anal sex possible. Condoms are always lubricated, but this lubrication alone is not enough. There are many lubricants you can buy for the purposes of anal sex and applying these will be necessary to make the experience tolerable for the woman.

Once you have covered all the bases, feel free to give anal sex a shot. Many people enjoy it, and some women claim to have very powerful orgasms from anal stimulation. Whether you will like it or not is up to you and refusing to have anal sex is perfectly fine, and the only major concern is that you keep clean and safe so as not to experience the issues mentioned.

Satisfying Your Partner's Fetish

Apart from the normal sexual practices listed above, there are many people who have certain special sexual desires, called fetishes. Fetishes can range from wanting to lick and admire your partner's feet, wanting to be watched while having sex or watching another couple have sex, all the way to having orgies with other couples or individuals or having sex in public places.

While no person is obligated in any way to give in to every desire their partner may come up with, finding a fetish you both enjoy can be extremely exhilarating. Even if you don't particularly enjoy a fetish your partner has, if it does not bother you, you should probably give in and let them experience it, as satisfying a person's fetishes is what will keep them more sexually interested in you than anything else.

There are some fairly disturbing fetishes, some of which may be caused by actual mental disorders, but most fetishes are simply buried sexual desires that can be satisfied quite easily and will make your partner enjoy your relationship even more.

Outercourse: Be Responsible

The outercourse, or heavy petting as some refer to it, is a practice often used by teenagers to experiment with their sexuality. While a couple or one of the partners may not yet be ready to go all the way and have intercourse, they may touch, caress and kiss each other's bodies and their various parts without actually having any type of sex, including oral, vaginal or anal.

This practice can still be very satisfying for the young couple and may lead to orgasms, as mutual masturbation can be just as pleasing as some forms of sex when done with care and by someone you are comfortable with.

One thing that is very important to be careful about is how far things go. Very often, young people get carried away and the phenomenon known as "date rape" may occur. What is meant here is that the two partners may be enjoying outercourse and get completely nude, and the outercourse may turn into intercourse without the girl actually consenting. While rape of any kind is extremely frowned upon, even illegal, this kind of a situation is very tricky as a girl getting into bed with a boy without her clothes on and fondling his genitals certainly bears a part of the responsibility in this kind of a scenario.

If you are a young person, make sure to remember to communicate. While the desire is strong and the hormones may take control many times, make sure that you talk to your partner about what they want and how far they are willing to go. For men, if you want to have intercourse with a girl for the first time, feel free to explicitly ask if it's alright with her. It may not be all that sexy, but it will make things clear and you won't be facing any consequences later in the case the girl was not ready and you just went for it.

Masturbating With a Partner: Keeping Safe from STDs

Masturbation is really the only form of sexual experience that will satisfy your need to orgasm while also keeping you 100% safe from STDs. More and more often, couples agree that instead of having sex, they will simply masturbate together. Masturbating each other can still spread some diseases, and really the safest way is for each partner to pleasure themselves with the other partner watching or touching them in other ways.

While this may seem a somewhat paranoid approach, many couples are afraid of STDs and the practice can be sexually enjoyable and fun for the couple. Watching porn together and masturbating can also be fun, as the very presence of the other person will certainly add some flare to an otherwise somewhat mundane activity.

While I personally find this practice a little too careful, I don't blame anyone for wanting to keep safe and I believe this practice is an intelligent and witty way of avoiding STDs with certainty while also having some sexual fun with your partner.

Chapter 6 –

The G-Spots

These are a real mystery to men, but they don't have to be. And even if women are complaining about not climaxing enough, it's as much their fault as it is their man's fault because they haven't taken the time to show their man where those particular points are and what they do. When you share this with your partner, you also let him know how to make you climax and go through the experience together. That's healthy sex.

The G spots are located, one on the outside of the vagina and the other deep within in. You need to experiment with your loved one and find out exactly where it is, as changing sexual positions may help you to locate it better. A rocking position is the best type and if you let her take charge and sit on you, she has the ability to move more and can position herself so that she is more likely to climax.

Broaching the subject of climaxes

For a man to approach a woman and ask if she has climaxed is like asking whether she likes chocolate. She will always say "yes" because woman have a caring nature and don't want to upset their man. However, if you tell her that you want to know where all her secret places are and take the time with foreplay, you will find out and this will enhance your sex life. She isn't likely to want to go to sleep as often if she knows that there is something very rewarding in it for her as well as for you.

Woman, especially in new relationships, generally don't want to hurt the man's feelings. Sex usually always feels good for the woman, so when lying about climaxing it may not feel like a "total" lie because the act of sex itself did feel great. Some men can be very sensitive when it comes to their penis, especially if they feel that they aren't comparable to other men. So much stigma lies on a man's endowment and if he feels he is below average he may be highly sensitive to any remarks or comments about it. It is general practice not to lie in the bedroom if you want to be with the person for a long period of time, but it is easy to get caught up in the moment and sometimes the easiest way to avoid confrontation during sex is to deal with the shortcomings not mention it. However, as a woman, it is your job to show the man what feels good to you and what you like being done to you to help you achieve an orgasm or to climax. Every woman is different so everyone ability to climax is different as well too.

If you find it hard to talk about things like that, don't talk. Just act. Ask her as you stroke her whether you have hit the right spot. Talk about sex openly and let her see that you don't mind that she hasn't got inhibitions. Women have this image in their heads that their man expects them to be white than white and won't often volunteer this information without prompting.

There is much controversy as to whether or not the Gspot actually does exist or not. Some people say it is easily found by placing your finger into the vagina and doing the "come here" motion with the finger. Some theorists say it is different for every woman because every woman is turned on by different factors. Some woman like pain so the positions that may be uncomfortable to some woman are enjoyable for others – and vice versa. This further heightens the mystery as to whether or not the Gspot is in an allotted place or if it is dependent on what the woman is aroused by.

You can even get her to show you. If she thinks that it's a wonderful turn on for you, she will oblige. Get her to touch the G spot on the outside and show you exactly where it is. You can even buy a vibrator for fun and tell her you want to tickle that spot.

One of the quickest ways to go about finding the Gspot is to look for it together. Have her direct your finger to the spot. Even searching for it during penetration can help you find the spot during intercourse. For men, many times you can tell where the spot is by the amount of moaning or other reaction from her. You can also feel as the vagina begins to excrete more fluids at a certain angle because this means the proper area is being aroused or stimulated. If a man never attempts to find or even asks the woman to show him where the Gspot is, there is really no other way for him to know other than the reaction you receive from her. For women, if you never show your man where the spot is by either actively engaging with him or by giving some type of reaction, you cannot expect him to know if he is pleasing you or not.

Where men tend to go wrong is that they don't talk about these things and then wonder why their women don't want sex as much as they do. The fact is that women like sex just as much as men do, but it has to be something that is mutually satisfying. Foreplay plays a huge part in that. The diagram below shows where these sensitive spots are:

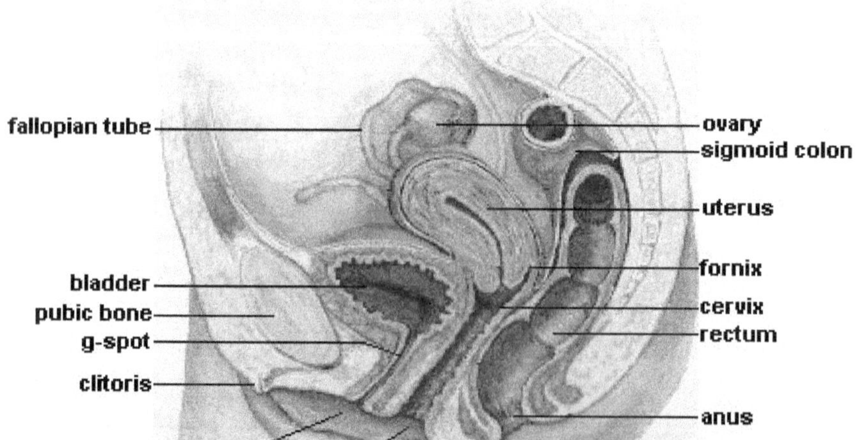

You can see that the actual G spot is inside the woman and sometimes when you are stimulating this, you need to bend your fingers to reach the right spot. Anal sex reaches it quite easily but if this isn't something you would consider then, try putting your fingers inside her and bending them backward toward the anus as you are much more likely to hit the right spot.

The clitoris on the outside of the vagina is another hot spot and is one that will help you to get her damp and stimulation of this really will turn her on. Fumbling won't. Be manly in your gestures and don't be afraid of it. She needs to feel definite stimulation, rather than schoolboy fumbling and if you start to feel her tense, do it even harder. If men have a hard time finding the clitoris, it is at the top of the vagina, usually beneath a fold of skin known as the "clitoral hood."

When it comes to the clitoris, every woman likes it stimulated differently. Once if becomes aroused by stimulation, it can become incredibly sensitive to the touch, making it almost unbearable if the man begins to become too rough with it. A lot of men believe that incessantly licking the clitoris is enough to make every woman climax and this could not be farther from the truth. Women need a variety of movements and efforts other than just licking. Gently kissing and sucking on the clitoris can be incredibly arousing.

With men, there are certain areas of the penis, such as the prostrate, that are more sensitive than others. Stroking the prostrate while performing oral sex on a man can greatly enhance the sexual pleasure, dependent on if the man is able to handle having a moving finger in his anus. A lot of men are weary of this exercise because it requires a finger in the anus, but relaxing and letting your significant other stroke your prostrate while sucking your dick can help the man reach a more euphoric climax.

Most people know how a penis works so I haven't gone into great detail about that. However, the parts that are most neglected during sex are the female parts that give her a climax and it is here that you need to practice the most. She won't object too much when she sees what it does to her because climax for a woman is very much as healthy and exhilarating as it is for a man. You just need to be aware that a woman has needs too and the less you care for those needs, the more likely it is that your love life will begin to fizzle out because quite frankly, one sided sex isn't much fun for her.

There are piles of videos on the Internet that you can watch together if you think that this will help your understanding of the female anatomy and the sooner you do understand it and give heed to it, the hotter your sex life will become.

Chapter 7 –
Getting in Tip Top Form for Sex

If you were going to run a marathon, you would prepare for it. You wouldn't expect to get it right and win with absolutely no experience at all. However, people go into sexual relationships and expect to get it right, regardless of what shape they are in. I had one client who came to me for advice whose wife was afraid to have sex with him because he had suffered a heart attack in the past and she did not want to become the cause of another. If you keep yourself fit, you also avoid this kind of worry. Your health matters, so make sure that you eat reasonable foods, that you keep your body relatively slim and that if you need supplements to help you, you take them.

Belly fat

No matter whether you are a woman or a man, belly fat can actually get in the way of great sex. You will not perform at your best if you have allowed your waistline to spread too much. You need to try and keep yourself fit. Although people do have sex when they have belly fat, there is much more likely to be inhibitions which stop that sex from being as good as it could be. Watch your diet and respect your body because this will help you to have better sex.

Not only is belly fat unhealthy, for men it can actually decrease the length of your penis due to the amount of fat buildup at the base. The more weight you lose, the extra fat at the base of the shaft falls off adding a few more centimeters to the length of the penis. For woman, the amount of fat buildup on the vagina can keep the man from maximum penetration because of the extra skin. With two overweight individuals, this causes even more of a problem because the man is already at a disadvantage from his excess fat and the addition of the woman's fat makes enjoyment more difficult.

It is hard to be flexible and hold your stamina when you have an excess amount of belly fat. Belly fat is an indicator of the shape that you are in and having a lot of it will slow you down and hinder your ability to try different, erotic sexual positions. Having fat that you have to lift in order to see or get to your genitals is a serious issue and should be addressed by a physician or a nutritionist before negative health effects being to arise.

Maximizing your potential

Before you prepare to go to bed, make sure that you have showered and that you smell nice. This works for both men and women and you may even want to take a shower together. Try to go to bed naked. It's much healthier and encourages skin to skin contact. Be careful that you have attended to things that may be a turn off. For example, if you have stubble on your chin, this may discourage her from wanting to nuzzle up to you. Similarly, a girl with stubble on her legs may just spoil the moment.

However, this is all dependent on the individual as some people find it attractive when they can smell the other person. It all depends on your partner and what they find arousing. It is always good practice to use proper hygiene to prevent any illness or infection if an injury is sustained during sex such as chafing, tearing, etc.

You need to look after your body and be really clean and healthy because it helps you to be sexy. Change your clothing often and always make sure that your underwear is particularly clean. Any odors in the area of your private parts is going to be a turn off and if you know yourself to have a problem, consult a pharmacy for the best soaps for this type of problem. Women also get vaginal itching or have problems with getting sufficiently lubricated for good sex. This can be overcome with creams. As far as the lubrication goes, if you are still young, then it is an indication that not enough foreplay was indulged in and you may need to encourage your partner to give you more attention before sex.

Oral sex

Oral sex can be considered one of the most pleasurable parts of the act of sexual intercourse. Not only is your partner able to focus directly on each individual area that they know you enjoy, but it also allows for exploration of each other's bodies which can help you bond and bring you closer together as a couple. Oral sex can be done before, during or after intercourse though it is typically almost always done before sex. Oral sex can be used as a form of foreplay and, if done correctly, can help each individual climax easily.

For men, oral sex is almost always expected or used to help get an erection and maintain it prior to penetration. Some men need constant stimulation orally, while other men are ok with a small amount. As a woman, know what your man wants and provide for him. This goes for men as well. Women need to pay very close attention when pleasing their man orally, being very careful not to accidentally use teeth or scrape the shaft of the penis. Woman can also use the testicles to their advantage as well by cradling them and gently fondling them in their hands. Lightly sucking and kissing the testicles can provide a great deal of pleasure as well. Again, we bring up the act of stroking the prostrate on the man by inserting a finger into his anus and gently stroking in a downward motion.

Woman should only perform this on a man if he is comfortable with it happening. Some men are uncomfortable at the thought of having a finger inserted into their anus. Woman can also engage in an act called "deep throating," which requires the woman to insert the penis into her mouth as far back as possible and begin to swallow. This can trigger the gag reflex if you are not well seasoned, so it should be done with caution if the woman is not familiar with the technique. Deep throating provides a great deal of pleasure of the man as the throat muscles massage his penis.

With women, oral sex tends to be less popular. Men have historically left the woman out in terms of oral sex for quite some time. There is a lot of speculation as to why this happens. Some woman do not enjoy oral sex being performed on them because they have never had it done correctly, some men are rough and oral sex can hurt, the vagina is a bit more complicated than the penis and its intimidating nature can cause men to shy away from pleasing it orally. As far as women go, orally pleasing a woman takes effort and passion. She can tell if you are not interested, the more passion you express the more aroused she will become.

Orally pleasing a woman can be done in several ways. Licking, kissing, and sucking on the clitoris that provide a great deal of satisfaction and pleasure. Combining the oral licking and sucking with a finger inserted into the vagina while doing the "come here," motion can send her into climax rather quickly. Licking the areas around the clitoris and inserting your tongue into her vagina occasionally can be arousing as well. As with any form of oral pleasure, make sure you and your partner are both on the same page to avoid any conflict and disagreements in the bedroom that could possibly kill the mood.

Know what your partner feels about oral sex. Perhaps you would like your lady to remove the hair in the pubic area and it is quite sex for her as well because it makes this area a lot more sensitive. If you think that would be a turn on, talk about it with her and see how she reacts. It will make oral sex a lot easier and this will act as a great lubricator for the sex that follows. If, however, she is against oral sex, then don't force this on her.

It can be very traumatic for a woman if she is afraid of oral sex. If, however, she is prepared to try it, make sure that you smell wonderful and that you are gentle with her and don't expect too much at first. She may not appreciate you climaxing in her mouth and if this is the case, you could talk to her about climaxing between her breasts that may be more acceptable to her.

Extra help in the way of stimulants

Although healthy people with a healthy appetite for sex shouldn't need too much help, there are certain foods and certain stimulants that can help you in your sex life. Capsaicin is one of the foods that gets you very sexy indeed because it is a hot food and stimulates the endings of the nerves. Thus, you feel more and your blood pumps faster, so that a meal at a restaurant known for dishes that use this may just be what you need to get yourself in the mood. Avocado and asparagus are not just posh foods. They help you to produce testosterone and other increases in hormonal activity that helps her. They can swell the clitoris and make sex very sensitive for her that will of course mean better sex for him as well.

Spinach is a vegetable that is rich in folate and helps with circulation. Improved circulation can help with arousal in the bedroom for both men and woman. Basil is another green food that can help blood flow through your body smoothly. When cooking, try to incorporate fresh basil and spinach wherever possible. Both plants are mild and can be used in a variety of different recipes.

Fox news posted an interesting article on a study that was done pertaining to watermelon and sex drive. "A 2008 article published by AgriLife Research maintains that when watermelon is consumed, citrulline is converted to arginine, an amino acid that impacts the circulation system. "The citrulline-arginine relationship helps heart health, the immune system, and may prove to be very helpful for those who suffer from obesity and type 2 diabetes," says Dr. Bhimu Patil, director of Texas A&M's Fruit and Vegetable Improvement Center. "Arginine boosts nitric oxide, which relaxes blood vessels, the same basic effect that Viagra has, to treat erectile dysfunction and maybe even prevent it".

Cayenne pepper in your food can help increase metabolism, heart rate, blood flow and sweat that can aid in the arousal of sexual advances. Although eating garlic is not recommended before a hot date due to the negative effects it has on the odor of your breath, garlic has also been known to provide extra sensitivity to our sexual organs due to increased blood flow. Resulting in obvious pleasurable effects.

Chocolates are a feel good food that also help you to get into a sexy mood, but don't overdo it. Overdoing the sugar intake may cause spikes in your sugar levels and that's not healthy, though a little chocolate in bed can be seen as a very healthy and sexy indulgence. Oysters are known to increase testosterone and to increase a man's sex drive. If you really want to end a meal with a sexy flavor, a glass of red wine will do the trick as this helps the blood flow and we all know that this is something that helps great erections to happen.

Chapter 8 –

Vitamins and Lifestyle Changes That Help Your Sex Drive

In the last chapter, we covered bases on things that you can do to make yourself ready for great sex, but there is help from the vitamin field as well that you may benefit from. If you are finding that you cannot last that long when you make love, you may want to consider some of these alternatives as they really will help you to have sex for longer. They do need to be taken on a regular basis to have effective results, but the list within this chapter will be helpful to those who feel that sex should be better than it actually is.

<u>Citrulline</u> – Although you may not be aware of this, this vitamin comes from the melon family and has been used for stamina for years. It isn't just used by people who want to increase the length of time that they can make love. It's also used by gymnasts and people who simply want to up their exercise so it will serve two purposes. Citrulline is nature's answer to Viagra, so if you would rather not discuss your love life with your doctor, you can buy supplements of L-cutrulline, but always respect the dosage as mentioned on the pack. Taking more of it won't improve your performance. It's not a bad supplement to take in general because it will also up your energy and that may just be what you need to feel great and to have sufficient energy at night to be sure of having a good time in bed.

<u>Vitamin E</u> is also a great vitamin to extend your love life into your later years. If you are middle aged and find that your libido is sinking fast, this is a good vitamin to take as it will help lift you out of that period toward feeling much more like having sex. Since vitamin E has many benefits both for men and for women, it's a little bit of a sneaky vitamin because you don't even have to mention that you are taking it to get your sex life into check! Popeye ate spinach for a purpose and eating spinach can also increase your intake of vitamin E.

Phenylalanine – This is something that is found in peanuts and all sorts of different foods such as almonds and pineapples. It is known as an aphrodisiac and if you are not eating these foods, you can buy supplements and take them daily. A daily dosage amount will depend upon the supplements that you purchase, so do respect the instructions given on the packet. Look also at contra-indications since you may be producing sufficient phenylalanine yourself and may not need it.

Magnesium, Zinc and Folic Acid – These are normally derived from your food, but you can buy vitamin tablets that will help the levels. Folic acid is important if you are trying for a baby since this can strengthen the sperm count.

The best way forward is to make sure that you have a varied diet and that it includes foods that produce all the vitamins and minerals that your body needs.

Lifestyle changes

One of the biggest problems when it comes to sex life is lack of sleep. You may think that people who don't sleep have more sex, but their bodies are unable to heal correctly. Sleep is essential to help all of the organs to regenerate and to heal after a day of work and it's vital that you have good quality sleep. If you are a victim of the times and find it hard to get quality sleep, try relaxation classes or even try lying down and listening to a relaxation tape before bedtime because this will help you to achieve the sleep that you need. If you are not getting a decent night's sleep, it will interfere with your sex life and it's important that you address this.

Sleep gives your body the ability to physically and mentally recuperate. Without proper sleep, you will begin to notice difficulties in all aspects of your life. It may not be obvious, but lack of sleep can cause irritability, mood swings, fatigue, aches and pains, and can cause a lot of unnecessary strain on your organs because while you are sleeping, your organs are resting as well. There are a lot of different ways to get your sleep in check. Your last resort should be medication because these have a lot of debilitating side effects and are not ideal to take over long periods of time. It is better to find a long-term solution to your problem by use of relaxation techniques, meditation, exercise, proper diet, and checkups to make sure everything else is healthy.

Overeating will also meddle with your love life, especially if you eat late at night. This can cause all kinds of problems because the digestion is not able to cope with this amount of food at night and you may find this is a reason why you are not sleeping correctly. Cut down the amount that you eat at night and make sure that you detox occasionally, to keep your digestive tract in good order. A great detox is to drink nettle tea. If you brew a whole pan full at a time and pour this into a plastic water bottle, you can drink it throughout the day and it will help you to detox, making your body feel less sluggish and encouraging you to be more inclined toward wanting sex!

Having energy can create a whole new sex drive you never thought you had. Overeating can hinder this energy so don't eat more than you need to feel full. Also, do not eat right before sex to avoid getting sick, the last thing you want is to get sick in bed. Overeating also leads to weight can which in turn, leads to belly fat. We have already discussed how belly fat can negatively affect your love life.

Drinking water is also important from the male and the female perspective. If helps you to keep your skin smooth and refreshed and it also helps your body to hydrate which will help you to be able to sustain sex for longer. These are habits that you need to employ if you want the best chance possible for your love life to keep going years into the future.

Lowering stress can help you in the bedroom as well. Having high amounts of stress can cause men to have difficulty ejaculating or getting and maintaining an erection. High amounts of stress in woman can cause her to be unable to climax because of the amount of thoughts and stressors on her mind. A lot of us do not realize the incredible effect on our health that stress has. It causes our muscles to tighten, making it more difficult to relax and get comfortable during sex. Being able to erase all other problems and just focus on sex can be difficult, but trying different outlets like exercise, meditation, yoga and pilates can all have a positive impact on your life.

Chapter 9 –
Great Sexual Positions for Her

In this chapter we are going to go into the positions that are best for her from several viewpoints. For example, if she likes to feel emotional attachment, then the positions that are chosen have been given as examples because they allow that intimacy that is important for a woman. Conversely, she may want a deep experience and this can be achieved by using the positions that are shown later in the chapter.

Emotional positions

These are important from a female point of view because she loves emotional security. A woman is driven by emotions. She needs to feel needed. She doesn't like to be used and certainly will not react well if there is not a little emotion mixed in with other sexual positions. Women like variety, but it is the emotional positions that will really win her over.

In the end though, most positions can be turned into emotional positions with the use of excessive rubbing, touching and kissing. For example, entering a woman from behind can feel very empty because you cannot see her face and her reactions. However, by reaching your hands around and cupping her breasts, kissing her back and lower back, and even gently pulling her hair can turn this seemingly shallow position into a position of great intimacy and emotion. You will get out of sex, what you put in, so keep this in mind. You cannot expect certain positions to come off as emotional if you are not willing to put the emotions into the positions.

If your woman is sleeping with her back to you, this is an ideal chance to cuddle up spoon fashion and to hold onto her breasts. She loves skin to skin and this is about as good as it gets. She will also feel if you want sex because this will be obvious and she has the choice of whether to respond or not. Don't expect a response that is favorable every time. Sometimes a cuddle is enough. However, if you don't get too masculine and push yourself on her, she is much more likely to be receptive and even encourage you to move so that you are inside of her.

This position is warm and loving and ideal for mornings when you wake up. It shows a great deal of respect for her and she will respond to it in a very positive way. It's also a great starter position that can easily lead to other positions that may be even deeper and more passionate. Kissing her gently on the back of the neck and licking her ear lobes can help with arousal if your end goal is penetration. Whispering sweet or dirty phrases and sayings in her ear can help to arouse her as well.

Another emotional position is the reversed missionary, because it puts her in control and you get to admire her body at the same time. This is a great position with her seated on top of you and in control. It shows a great deal of trust on the part of the man and he should encourage her to do what she will! What he is accepting when he encourages this position is that he sees her as an equal and that's very important in this day and age. It isn't all about him. It's about both of them and this position says he is open to that kind of thinking.

Crisscross is a wonderful position that allows for easy access to the woman clitoris, usually requiring stimulation in order to achieve an orgasm. Crisscross is when the woman lies on her back and the man lies beside her on his side. She drapes her legs over him in an "x" position, allowing him to enter her from behind. This also gives him easy access to caress her breasts or kiss her, allowing for deeper connections during sex.

The coital alignment technique is said to be the "greatest sex position in the world" because of the close physical connection and the best clitoral stimulation. This position is started in normal missionary position but is then transitioned by the man leaning forward and putting all of his weight onto her. He is this supposed to move himself forward until the base of his penis (also known as the pubic bone) is touching her clitoris. The woman then wraps her legs around the man's thighs and they move together in a rocking motion.

The ankles-up position involves the woman being on her back with the man in front, like the missionary position. From here, instead of him leaning forward, he is going to stand straight up and grab each of her ankles with his hands. Holding onto the ankles, he is going to then thrust himself into her. This allows for great depth and a visually stimulating picture for the man.

Positions that will give depth

There are several positions that give extra depth and if a man is smaller, or worries about his size, then these are probably going to be the best for him as well. If you start with the spoon position and then move so that he is kneeling behind her, this position gives him great access and means that he can get deeper. That means that he will feel more but it also means that he is more likely to reach those places that women really need the man to, in order to achieve climax.

Using a pillow can also help with deeper penetration and maintaining pleasure. A pillow can either be placed under her stomach while participating in doggy-style, or underneath her lower back when participating in missionary. This elevation provided by the pillow allows for deeper penetration and a great visual for the man as well. There is easy access to the clitoris for either the man or the woman, and both parties have an amazing view of each other.

Another position that is good starts with missionary position or reversed missionary with either him or her on top. If she is on top, then he rolls her over so that she is beneath him and then moves away a little so that he can grab her legs and place her ankles onto his shoulders. This too is a very deep experience and she will certainly appreciate that because it means that both are satisfied. If you are doing this for the first time, and you are well endowed, take it slowly at first because she may not be accustomed to that depth and it takes a little while to become accustomed to it. Too harsh a movement may hurt her. Remember that her participation is as important as yours. If you are going to try deep sex, then make sure that she is aware of how deep you are going to go. She may, on the other hand, encourage it and pull you toward her so that she takes everything that you have.

Having her bend over and spread her legs apart slightly, allowing him to enter her while he is on his knees behind her, gives a great deal of depth as well. Entering from this position can be done rough or gently depending on the needs and wants of the woman, always enter gently initially to avoid injury.

Having the man sit on the edge of a chair or a solid object, then having the woman sit on his lap facing him provides deep penetration. The woman can take control or she can stand on the balls of her feet and have him take control, whichever the couple prefers. This position can also incorporate a great deal of kissing, making it more passionate, because you are face to face with one another.

A position called the butterfly is done when a woman lays on her back with her legs spread apart. The man is standing and enters her from the front. She then angles her hips upward and places a pillow or a blanket to help keep her hips elevated. The man continues to enter her this way, allowing for maximum penetration.

Shyness

Respect a woman who is shy and take it slowly. She may have self-image problems and it will take her a while to trust that you love her just the way that she is. Never make her endure being vulnerable. Instead, it is better to encourage nakedness slowly until she reaches a time when it is no longer a problem. Then, you really can explore each other's bodies without inhibitions getting in the way. If you try to take it too quickly in a situation like this, you may frighten her, which may make future lovemaking episodes even more difficult. It's important to gain her trust. You have to appreciate that women are shy for different reasons. Some – it's just a question of body image. With others – they may have experienced something that frightened them in the past and will need your help and understanding to overcome their fears.

Some women are taught that sex is a man's game and to abide by his wants and needs. Some women are taught not to cater to a man's needs in the bedroom, but to instead focus on what each of you has to offer. Being shy in the bedroom can be a mixture of how one was raised along with how comfortable one is in her own skin. When dealing with a woman who is shy, compliment her often and tell her everything you love about her. Tell her she has nothing to be shy about and encourage her. Different women come from different backgrounds. There is no telling what caused her to feel shy about being in the bedroom.

Chapter 10 –
Great Sexual Positions for Him

You may be surprised that there are positions that are clear leaders both for women and for men, but for different reasons. A reverse missionary, with her on top, is actually the number one position for a man. He puts her in control and you may think that men don't like that, but you would be wrong. If she is taking the lead, she is pleasing herself, but she is also freeing up his hands, so that he can enjoy her contours. That's important to a man. He can fondle her breasts and enjoy himself and when he wants to take control, it's very easy from this position by simply flipping her over!

Missionary position, although fairly boring if done too often can also be very passionate for a man who likes to take control. He loves the skin to skin contact. It gives him the animal feeling of being in control and that's a natural state for a man to feel good in, especially in bed. Not only that, he can feel her hips pushing toward him and can allow him to pull her toward him so that lips can lock in passion. Some people love that closeness and a man likes to feel he has his woman ready to kiss, to hold, to fondle and to love and this position gives him it all. It isn't as dull as some may suppose, because it gives a man a lot of thrust. It's an easy position for him to use his full thrust to fill her and to feel her responding to him.

If you are going to do the missionary position, be aware that men hate resistance and sometimes this is a position that seems to encourage that. You need plenty of foreplay because if he cannot enter you, he will find it frustrating. Thus the foreplay should be encouraged so that there is no difficulty at all entering the vagina. It's also a fallacy that men only like this position because it gives them control. Yes, they do have control, but they also like their woman to move in harmony with them, rather than just lying there letting them do all the work.

In intimate positions such as these, the aroma of the skin is vital to the situation because odors really can put a man off. Make sure that you have bathed. Make your skin soft with oils and also make sure that you breath is superbly fresh. There is nothing worse than a man leaning forward to kiss a woman who smells like last night's ashtray.

Doggie style allows a man to give more thrust and to be in control. This is the position that also gets him deepest inside her. He also gets a great view of her and can see himself entering her vagina, so that this works as a stimulation to make him feel even sexier. How the woman controls the situation is by placing herself in such a position that she gains a little control as well and can tease him a little to make the lovemaking last longer. In fact, if he wants her to, she can do as much thrusting as she lives taking in as much of his penis as she feels that she is comfortable with. That makes it a win win position for both the man and the woman. The only snag with this position is that it does encourage the man to climax early, so it's better to start in another position and to move into this position for the finale, by which time both man and woman will be ready for that violent thrust and can enjoy joint climaxes if they get it right.

Most men have fantasies about quickies and although this isn't what people should do all of the time, the naughtiness involved in a quickie really will turn him on and drive him crazy. Whether this is against a wall, over a table or sneaked in when no one is suspecting it, the naughtier the action, the more the turn on. It has to be naughty. It has to be quick and it has to feel good for both. Thus, expect it to be over quickly, but expect it to be both violent and crazy because it will be. This gives a man a great sense of control but it also shows him how naughty his woman is prepared to be.

The 69 position is a favorite for men who love oral sex. It puts both in control of the other's climax and if you go by the old Kama Sutra belief that sex isn't about you, it's about pleasure to your partner – then this position really does work to do that. Both of you are giving each other pleasure. However, there are snags with this position. If she has hair, then perhaps this would put you off, and if may be a good thing to encourage her to remove it, though never encourage this in a way that makes her feel like she is lacking in some way. Introduce the subject and say how you think it would be if she had no hair. Similarly, a woman may not like him climaxing in her mouth and may be shy about it and in a case such as this, you can turn at the last minute and penetrate her so that the climax happens inside her and you both feel the benefit of it.

Men and women have different preferences because of the way that they are built. The reverse cowboy is favored by some men, because he can see her but he can also see himself entering her, which is a great turn on. If you try these positions, you won't go far wrong and the naughtier the nicer. Men like to know that their women are fully involved in sex and are enjoying it as much as they are.

Chapter 11 –
Why Dialog is Important

If you were having a one off sexual situation with a stranger, then silence might do you both a service, but in the case of sex with a regular partner, dialog is what helps the sexual experience grow. You get to know what you both like. You get to talk about your fantasies and may even get to live them. The kind of problems that can occur if the dialog is not there are:

- She may reject his initiation for reasons of her own which he may misunderstand
- She may never initiate sex because she is worried about what her partner may think of her
- He may never indulge in foreplay because she hasn't said she wants it
- He may not know where her sensitive spots are because they have never really discussed it
- They may never know each other's fantasies and miss an opportunity to fulfill them

There are many relationships that hit muddy water because of lack of dialog. She didn't want sex because she was feeling ill. He automatically thought that she was rejecting him and got to a situation where he no longer initiated sex. She thought she was unloved. It's a typical scenario where dialog would have made the difference. It is situations like this that lead to misunderstandings that may even lead to a relationship breaking up. We often see on TV the man who wants sex but whose wife does not. We also see girls laughing together about the fact that men have no idea what turns them on.

Dialog allows all this. The introduction of porn isn't necessary, but some couples find that it breaks the ice and allows them to talk about things that they would otherwise find impossible. "We watched someone having anal sex," explained one lady, "and the woman seemed to be enjoying it immensely, so we thought we would try it." Her husband actually enjoyed it because it was a very tight experience and as she had given birth to kids over the years, she had lost the elasticity of the vagina. Having anal sex allowed them both to rediscover pleasures they hadn't experienced for a while.

Anal sex can be a great way to explore and experiment with one another to see what each of you likes and dislikes. Some men are completely opposed to anything anal related whereas other men fantasize over it. Depending on your desires, anal sex should be practiced carefully and with a large amount of lubrication to avoid ripping or tears. Condoms should also be worn to reduce the incidence of infection for both parties involved. Anal sex can be highly enjoyable for both women and men and can be extremely desirable when combined with vaginal or clitoral stimulation.

"He wanted me to dress in suspenders and sexy underwear," said one woman after talking to her husband about his fantasies. She actually changed her priorities. She had always given priority to the clothing that people see but not to the underwear she wore. When she did, it actually improved her attitude too, because she felt very sexy and they both enjoyed the experience.

It is incredibly important to talk to one another about your sexual fantasies. There is no reason why you should keep these to yourself and why you both shouldn't entertain the others sexual fantasies every so often. Once married, having to spend a lifetime keeping your sexual fantasies hidden could lead to potential problems in the future, talking and sharing keeps you both in the loop and aware of what the other one wants.

"My husband loved to make love out in the open" said another woman. "It was a fantasy of his." She explained that they had found a way that they could do this and that out in the garden with skin against the warm summer evening grass, they found their fun in sex again, even though they had lost this years beforehand.

Having sex out in the open or in nature can been very animalistic and raw. One of the reasons we as humans enjoy it so much is because it's the way our ancestors used to make love; its engrained in our history, it's instinctual. What is most interesting about having sexual intercourse outside is how widely practiced it is. Yet you never see it taking place (which is the idea, you certainly do not want to get caught having sex in public). Most people assume they are the only ones doing it, though this is hardly the case. Having sex in the water is also pleasurable for some, though for women who have problems with lubrication, it can cause problems if you wish to continue the session outside of the waters.

The dialog between a couple in bed is every bit as important as the dialog that they enjoy during the day. If your partner does not know what your fantasy is, how can he/she fulfill it? That's why many couples do open up and try to discuss different things about sex, so that they can experiment and have fun with sex. It's something that couples shouldn't shy away from because this dialog allows them to get to know each other better and to cater for each other's deepest desires.

Just speaking to one another about each other's wants and desires can bring your relationship to whole new level. Being comfortable enough around your significant other to explained to them what you want and what you are or aren't getting can keep conflict and distress from building up and taking away from your sexual enjoyment as a couple. Communication in any relationship is number one. You can't hide things from your partner that bother you, and expect them not to boil over in the future.

Never tried tantric massage? This is a real eye opener and if you haven't tried it yet, wait for an evening when you know you will have no interruptions and give it a try. This is where oils are used to rub against the sensitive areas of the body and huge climaxes can be reached using this method. While the massage is going on, the dialog between you is also part of the picture and believe me, it's going to be very sexy indeed. The idea of this type of massage is total pleasure and if you can go into it with open eyes and a good dialog with your partner, you should be able to explain the tingling sensations that happen and give your partner a great indication of places that are touched which give the most pleasure. This dialog all helps you to discover each other's bodies and enjoy your sex together.

If she has a headache, don't read into it. A headache is a temporary hiccup. If you see it as a rejection, it means that the lack of dialog between you is getting in the way of your love life. Talk to each other, understand each other and never be afraid of experimenting together. You may even find new ways to make love that you never dreamed of but which happen as a consequence of your bedtime discussions. In fact, if the headache is tension related, sex might help to alleviate the headache because sex released endorphins which can counteract the effects of cortisol, a hormone that is released during large amounts of stress.

Chapter 12 –
Keeping Your Sex Life Steaming Hot

The intimacy that is felt by a couple doesn't have to come to a grinding halt the moment you hit difficult situations. It should always be there. You need to keep it alive. A woman can send a sexy text to her husband giving him a promise of what's to come when he gets home, but a man can do sexy things too. He can bring home a bottle of wine and a sexy pair of panties any time he wants to and insist on her modeling them for him. It's all about adoring each other. The moment you stop that adoration; your love life becomes stunted.

Remember – she's the sentimental and emotional one

Women are always receptive to sex if their emotional needs are dealt with. They love flowers, they love flattery, and they love being loved. If a woman feels loved, she will try anything that you want to try and it's important to remember that. Let her feel used and miserable, and your love life will dry up faster than an oasis in the desert on a hot day. The problem is that while men don't need this kind of emotional commitment, women do. Adore her, love her, shower her with love and expect a hot return. She will be available to make love in the shower when you come in from work. She won't mind making love on the rug in front of the fire. She won't even mind showing you what she does with her vibrator and letting you have a go. Forget about her emotional needs and you set yourself up for disappointment.

Make her feel beautiful. Take photos of her. Touch her and encourage her to tell you where to touch her. Run your fingers over her skin and feel her body react. Your fingers will tell you when there is a reaction. Tell her you love her because she is so receptive to your touch. Remember the emotional link when you are dealing with a woman. A woman who feels secure and loved won't mind being the vamp occasionally when you want animal sex, but if you forget her emotions, she will tell you where you can go to get that type of relationship. She demands respect and if she doesn't get it, she's hardly likely to fall in with your image of bondage or making love in the park. That respect and emotion is central to everything that you do with her.

Remember – He is a driven animal

Your man may be a perfect gentleman. He may be your idea of masculinity. He may treat you with respect but when it comes to his actions in bed, a man will be thinking with a part of his anatomy that isn't located in his head. His hormone levels will rise and being the hunter of the human race, he will be trying to get what he wants. That doesn't mean that a man won't respond to kind and loving love-making. What it does mean is that the sentimental side of it may not be as important to him as it is to her. However, if he is kind and loving, he is liable to respond to her needs.

The man's aim from sex is to have a great erection, to feel driven and to eventually have a wonderful climax. Thus, quit your whining. He doesn't want to know about what you think about the next door neighbor, how the cat bit you or whether someone on Facebook upset you – at least not when it's time for bed. You need to understand that for him, it's sex pure and simple and although he loves you, he needs you to concentrate on sex so that it's good for both of you.

This is why it is a good idea to leave all electronics outside of the bedroom and refrain from having a television in your room. If the television must stay, keep it off at night time as it can be distracting during sex and bonding time. When it is time for bed, everything else needs to be put away, climb into bed and focus on one another and not anything else that may be going on social media wise or television wise. This can also be said for any time you are out and about, spending time with one another. Spend time with each other, not looking at your phone or social media.

One thing that one couple found was a middle ground. They were able to talk during sex and had a great laugh through doing that. Their relationship was the strongest I have ever come across and this seemed to be because she didn't overly demand emotional stuff when he was trying to strut his animal stuff. Their lives seemed to be in synch and they had a great love life right up to their senior years.

When you remember the masculine needs and also respect the feminine needs, you find that your love life can be electric. It's like being on the same page and in the same place at the same time. There's a certain decorum about your sex life and if you cross the lines, and get it wrong, boy do you get it wrong! Thus, for men to make the most of sex, remember her emotional needs. For women to make the most of sex, remember his animal needs and steer him to understanding your bodily needs. From the video that we showed you at the beginning of this book, it would seem that most males do need that extra bit of education when it comes to knowing which of your buttons to press.

Men need to remember that she's emotional. She has hormonal problems once a month and during this time, it is best that you simply cuddle up and make her feel loved. If you can put away your animal instincts and do this, she will love you all the more for it.

Toys

The introduction of sexual toys into the bedroom can help to spice alive between the sheets. There are hundreds of different sex toys to use in the bedroom, which might be of a surprise to people who are used to the vanilla form of sex. Starting off with a few of the most well-known sex toys, the vibrator coming in as the most well-known. Dildos are the form of vibrators that do not vibrate, both toys come in the shape of a penis, torpedo – anything relatively similar to those shapes. These shapes can also be angled upward to better reflect the natural penis. Vibrators and dildos are easy to use and offer pleasure for both the men and women alike. Dildos specifically created for anal play are also available.

Focusing on the anal region, there are a few different types of toys that can be introduced and used that pertain to the anal cavity. One thing to keep in mind when venturing into the anus is that, anatomically, the anus is not designed to have anything inserted into it. The anus is, more or less, a one-way freeway for our excrement. Due to this fact, you need to be extra careful when inserting and playing in this area. Only use toys that are specifically designed for the anus and never let go of any toy that has been inserted more than 75% of the way in because the anus acts as a vacuum and will suck up any objects that are left. Seems strange when the anus is supposed to only be one way, however the muscles are the same muscles that help keep your feces in when you don't have a place to use the restroom.

Also, be careful to always use lubrication as tearing and rips can easily occur and are prone to infection because of the area they are located. Although it is rare you would get sick from your own bacteria in your colon, it is always better to stay on the safe side. Lubrication should also be the kind intended for intercourse and nothing toxic or intended for other uses.

The first toy we will go over is the butt plug. The butt plug is shaped like a like a wine stopper and is inserted into the anus like a plug; hence the name. The reason butt plugs are used during intercourse is because some individuals find it pleasurable to have something in their anus during sexual intercourse or masturbation. For couples that are planning to engage in anal sex, a butt plug can help relax the muscles surrounding the rectum that makes the process of insertion into the rectum easier. Butt plugs come with a flared end so that once inserted, there is a low risk that the plug will be sucked into the bowels.

Another sex toy that is designed to be inserted into the rectum is anal beads. These beads are balls linked together on a chain with a flared or handle end so they don't get sucked into the rectum. These beads are used to help enhance sexual intercourse by adding pressure in the rectum and euphoric sensations upon insertion and removal. These toys can be used by either men or women and come in a variety of sizes and lengths.

Focusing on the men now, there are a few different types of toys that cater to you. There is a toy called the "penis ring," which is a ring that is inserted at the base of your shaft, behind or in front of your testicles, depending on size, preference, and the type you purchased. The rings help men who have a difficult time staying full erect but constricting blood flow in the penis, making it stay harder for a longer period of time. These rings benefit both women and men for obvious reasons; woman get to the enjoyment of a strong and lasting erection and the man gets to enjoy himself and the pleasure he is giving to the woman. The penis rings are also available ribbed, plastic, rubber, and vibrating. The vibrating penis rings can add even more pleasure for the man, allowing the woman to feel slight vibrations through the penis.

More sex toys geared towards men are prostrate toys that can be inserted into the anus and made to vibrate on the prostrate. These toys are usually shaped like a long rod with an egg shape at the end. Men can insert these themselves or the can have their significant other do so during oral or penetrative sex. Other sex toys for men do exist, though they are largely based on single masturbation so they would not be appropriate for this section.

For woman, along with the vibrators and other items mentioned above, there are a few more toys that can be added to sex to enhance pleasure. One of these toys is the "G spot vibrator" which is similar in shape to the male prostrate vibrator, however it is angled slightly different to accommodate the female vaginal anatomy. This can be used during anal intercourse to help the woman climax during anal sex.

There are also clitoral vibrators that can be used during vaginal or anal sex, helping with arousal and stimulation of the clitoris. It can be difficult for some woman to climax during vaginal intercourse. That is why toys like these can help solve that problem. They can be held by either the man or the woman during intercourse, whichever is most comfortable.

Bonding without sex to create better sex

Bonding with one another outside the bedroom can seem like an impossible task for some. Traditionally, we get up, go to work, come home, eat and spend time together in the form of television, games, or reading. Sometimes this time is spent in separate rooms before going to bed. Once in bed, this should turn into your bonding time as a couple. You are so busy and tired during the day it's hard to even have the desire to put effort into your stagnant relationship. This not only causes damage to your relationship over time, but it also has a huge impact on your sex life. If you don't find one another desirable even when you are exhausted, something needs to be done.

There are a bunch of small, erotic things you can do with one another that will echo into the bedroom and help to spice up your sex life. A seemingly strange yet surprisingly fun act is the male shaving the woman's legs. This can be seen as erotic and relaxing for the woman and pleasing to the man because he gets to touch her rub her smooth legs. It will bring you closer to one another and help you notice things about one another you may have missed. Depending on taste, the man can also shave the woman's pubic region. Perhaps he wants to try something new and shave it bald or leave a strip or a patch of hair? Allowing him to take control of your body can be seen as incredibly erotic to the man while also giving a feeling of pampering from the woman.

Taking bathes together can be very sensual. Depending on size, it may be difficult to fit both of you in the tub at one time, but if it is possible to fit, take advantage of it. With the man in back and the woman placed in-between his legs, pressed up against his penis, he can wrap his arms around her and play with her breasts and kiss her neck. Soaking in the warm water together and enjoying touching one another is highly erotic and can lead to other sexual acts later on in the night.

Cuddling on the sofa or chair together when watching television can be a huge act of intimacy. Instead of sitting apart or across from one another, slide next to one another in a lying position and gently rub one another. This is especially important after a long day at work because you have been away from one another all day. Even giving each other a small hand massage while watching television can get someone into the mood and help them to relax. It is all about the little things in relationships that help build up the desire to be with one another sexually. Cuddling should never be ignored.

Going for walks together after work can bring you closer together as well. Instead of coming home and engaging in other tasks to mindlessly staring at the television, go for a walk together outside and talk about your days. You may be surprised at what the other has to say. This can help bring you together and bond with one another while also engaging in physical activity. Even talking with one another on a walk about having sex later can get you both excited, especially since the blood is already flowing from your walk. Never ignore the benefits of physical activity on your mental, physical, and sexual states and relationships.

Having a date night where each of you dresses up in some of your nicest clothes. The woman gets all dolled up with her makeup and outfits and perfume, the man wears his best cologne. Make the bed (if not already done in the morning) before you leave so you can come home to a more picturesque bedroom. Spend the evening chatting and have one drink, one appetizer, split an entrée and share a dessert. Sharing meals can help you realize how much you care for each other and how much you enjoy sharing not only your food with them, but your life. When coming home and preparing to get undressed, spend a few moments passionately or gently kissing on the bed before beginning the process, this might lead you to some sexual excitement before preparing for bed.

Spend one weekend morning cooking breakfast with one another. Spending time with one another doing simple, everyday tasks and enjoying one another's company is one of the best parts about being in a relationship. Being best friends and wanting to spend all your free time with your significant other – that is why you picked each other right? It can be difficult to make time for tasks like this, especially if you both have different schedules. You have to make time if you want the relationship and the sexual energy to continue. Caring for one another and showing that you care will reflect into the bedroom.

These tasks may not seem like they would make much of an impact on couples who have been together for a long time, but you would be surprised to know how much of an impact it does have. Being with someone for a long time and having sex with someone for long periods of time can begin to seem monotonous. You or the other may desire less and less time with one another because you "see each other all the time" when the reality it you don't. You may see each other, but you don't look at each other. You don't admire one another.

These tasks help you to go back in time and see what drew you to the person you are with. It is easy to think you are spending time with one another when you really aren't. There is no talking, just being in each other's presence. Now, don't assume that every minute spent with one another needs to be filled with mindless chatter because it doesn't. Being in each other's presence is a wonderful thing when do occasionally, but day in and day out of sitting with one another and not having a meaningful conversation about one's feelings on certain issues can begin to harden a relationship and make you resent one another.

Never overlook the small stuff because, like I said before, a bunch of small stuff can lead to a boiling over. Talk to one another, spend time with one another, touch one another and you may be surprised the impact it has on your sex life.

For couples who have not been together as long as others, or for couples who are not yet married, this time if for exploration and learning about each other's wants and desires. You are not committed to one another under vows (as you are with marriage) so you can use this freedom to express yourself sexually and freely and see what is accepted by your partner. If your significant other does not accept or approve of your desires, then you have the freedom to search elsewhere. You commit to someone that you could see yourself having a healthy sexual, emotional and physical relationship with for the rest of your life, not someone you have to "settle" for.

Edibles

Being adventurous in the bedroom can be done with more than just toys and costumes. There are other ways to be equally as exciting while also enjoying some sweet treats as well. There are edible items of clothing that are made of different candies that can be worn by either the man or the woman. The other partner will then bite the candies off and feed them to you or nibble at them and eat them, teasing the other. This can build the anticipation for the act of sex to occur, or the buildup of foreplay.

Edibles can also be in the form of whipped cream or chocolate syrup (among other things) these are some of the most commonly known of the edibles. You can place the edibles anywhere on the body, if you are a man placing, for example, whipped cream on the woman, there are a few spots in which you should pay close attention to. Placing some on the clitoris and vaginal area can be arousing, as well as placing a line down her stomach for you to eat off. You can also place whipped cream on her nipples because the nipples are a very sensitive region. There may be other areas she wants you to place the whipped cream so it is all up to you.

If you are a woman placing, for example, chocolate syrup on a man, you may focus on similar areas that the man did for the woman. Placing syrup at the base or the tip on the penis and licking it off can be arousing, along with placing syrup on the testicles and gently licking and sucking the syrup off. You can also draw a line or squiggles with the syrup and trace the lines with your tongue. This can be fun for the guy if you give him the chocolate syrup and let him make a trail where he wants you to go and you trace it with your tongue. It is also arousing to have the nipples licked, even for the man. Placing a drop of chocolate syrup on his nipples and sucking it off can be incredibly arousing.

Chocolate has been known to be an aphrodisiac, which is why it is offered in a lot of different forms for sex. There is a chocolate dusting powder than can be dusted onto the skin and licked off, along with chocolate syrup and chocolate candies on edible clothing. There are other forms of edibles as well, including flavored condoms for couples who use them during intercourse or for oral sex. The flavored condoms help to mask the latex taste and feel in your mouth, making the use of them a bit more pleasurable.

You can use candies for other uses than edible underwear or clothing. You can use them to make a trail, along the same lines at the chocolate syrup, and either suck or gently use your teeth to eat them off of your partner. This can be arousing because the delicate touch of your lips and teeth on their skin can build up anticipation of what is to come. Candies of all kinds can be used, along with different kinds of chocolate.

The use of ice cubes can be enjoyable as well. When we get excited and aroused, we naturally heat up. Using ice cubes can be arousing and stimulating because it counteracts the heat. The contrasting temperatures can be highly enjoyable. You can use the ice cube by keeping it in your mouth and poking it out each time you kiss your significant other in different areas. You can also place the ice cube on their stomach and use your finger to push the ice cube around their body, grazing other the nipples and over the penis or vagina quickly. You do not want to hold the ice cubes on your private areas for too long because there are a large amount of nerve endings and the pleasurable experience can quickly become painful if not careful.

Role-playing is also a wonderful way to keep things exciting in the bedroom. Sometimes, having sex with the same person can become boring for some, and there are ways to change this by losing yourself in a world of imagination. You can both take on different personas, even dress differently than you normally would. Some couples act out affairs while others pretend to be two strangers who met in a bar. There are thousands of different scenarios to choose from. Having the guy come home from work pretending to be the mailman, the garbage man, the mechanic – any of those things can be arousing.

The point of roleplaying is to take on new roles and give the impression that you are having a sexual encounter with someone other than your normal sexual partner.

Role-playing can also be used to help the other person pretend to be something they aren't, like an animal or a person of a different gender. Role-playing can really help some people express their imagination through sex and depending on your partner, it can get a little bit overwhelming. When beginning the act of roleplaying, each choose a roll that is similar to their current persona, just to help warm up. It might even be a good idea to start off with only one of you roleplaying.

Chapter 13 –
Safety First

Sex is one of the most enjoyable human experiences without a doubt, and enjoying it openly and freely is something many generations did not have the privilege of doing, which is why we should appreciate it all the more. Sex can also be dangerous in many ways and it can't be stressed enough how important safety is during sexual encounters.

Adults who practice sex in the modern world should already be more than well- informed on the topics of sexually transmitted diseases (STDs) and unwanted pregnancies, but the importance of these things is so great it should not be left out of this book. In fact, it could be that practicing safe sex is the most important part of sexual education, as failing in all other aspects of sex will only cause temporary problems. Failing to keep sex safe may cause irreparable damage in form of STDs or cause pregnancy when it is not expected or wanted.

Sexually Transmitted Diseases

Having sex with multiple partners may sound like a ton of fun, and it can be, but it can also be pretty dangerous. There are currently over 30 common sexually transmitted diseases, some of them incurable and the more partners you change, the bigger the possibility of getting infected with one. One in four American adults who is currently alive will contract at least one STD in their lifetime and you want to make sure you are in the other three if you can help it.

Not every potential partner will have an STD and choosing the right partners to have sex with will be a big part of keeping safe from STDs. Some groups of people, such as those addicted to intravenous drugs such as heroin, will often have a higher chance of having

STDs as opposed to those who take good care of their overall health and have regular medical checkups. Also, people who have had fewer sexual partners will have a lower chance of being infected with an STD than those who have changed partners many times.

The symptoms of STDs are not always easily visible as some people, especially women, will often not exhibit any obvious signs of an STD at all. Others may only experience slight fevers or other symptoms that they cannot connect with an STD in any real way. This is why it will be difficult to actually know if someone is infected with an STD, but assessing the risk should play a big part in choosing sexual partners.

The simplest way of preventing STDs is quite obvious: don't have sex! But this is clearly not what this manual is written for, so your next best option is to have sex with a single partner who you know well and you know or are fairly certain is STD-free. Even still, using protection is advisable, as contracting an STD is not something that can be taken care of with any kind of magic. In fact, some STDs, such as AIDS are deadly and incurable, so keeping safe of those will be a very important part of your sexual life.

Here are a few of the more common diseases to be on the lookout for and keep safe from:

Chlamydia

Chlamydia is one of the most common STDs in the world, with millions worldwide being infected by it at some point in their adult lives. It is easily transmitted and causes various symptoms in men and women. In women, Chlamydia can be hard to detect as it does not manifest in a visible way very often. In the long term, the disease may cause a woman to become sterile, experience ectopic pregnancy and pelvic pain.

In men, Chlamydia will cause painful urination within days of getting infected and may cause testicular swelling, which can be very painful. Fortunately, Chlamydia is very treatable with antibiotics, but can be hard to properly diagnose, which is why going to the doctor as soon as you experience any of these symptoms will be of extreme importance.

Gonorrhea

Gonorrhea is the second most common STD in the US and the world, with millions of reported, and likely just as many unreported, cases. Many patients who are infected with gonorrhea never even experience any symptoms and those who do may often not recognize them for what they really are.

The symptoms of gonorrhea may include yellowish discharge from the vagina, frequent urination, swelling of the vulva and other tenderness in the genitals. The disease can be spread through all forms of sex, including anal and oral, and in the long run Gonorrhea can cause severe issues if left untreated, such as arthritis and issues with the cardiovascular and central nervous systems.

Fortunately, gonorrhea can also be treated with penicillin and other antibiotics, and is often treated together with Chlamydia as people often get infected by both at the same time and the treatment is similar.

Herpes

Another well-known STD, herpes is caused by the Herpes Simplex virus and is incurable. On the surface, herpes appears in the form of a rash with white blisters on top, which can appear on a person's genitals, mouth, anus and other body parts. Millions of people around the world suffer from herpes and while the disease is not very dangerous, it is not pleasant either, and you will want to warn any partners of it before engaging in sex.

In cases where a woman is infected with herpes, the disease can cause miscarriages during pregnancy and sores in the vaginal area during childbirth may cause serious health issues to the baby, which is why women with herpes should opt for a C-section.

Herpes is not always visible, but if you experience inexplicable sores and rashes, often in the mouth region, it is possible you have herpes and you should see a doctor about it. If you do have herpes, you should always warn your partner and should not engage in sex without using a condom. Even a condom will not protect your partner 100% so make sure your partner knows what they are getting into before doing it. Herpes is very common nowadays and you should not be ashamed of it in any case, and keeping healthy and safe is much more important than keeping face.

Syphilis

Syphilis first came to Europe in the 15th century from either America or Africa, and caused a major epidemic which killed hundreds of thousands and created a major scare among the European population. The disease is caused by tiny microscopic organisms called Treponema Pallidum and can resemble all sorts of other diseases, often making it hard to diagnose.

Syphilis comes in three stages. In the first stage, right after infection, the disease will manifest at the very site of invasion, either around the genitals, lips, tongue or anus. It will appear in the form of a chancre, which is a painless sore that goes away after some time.

The second phase of syphilis appears once the disease has spread through your bloodstream and reached all the tissues of the body. In this phase, a patient will experience painless rashes anywhere on their body which will go away after a while on their own without leaving scars. These are not dangerous but are indicative of the spread of syphilis and one should absolutely seek medical help if such symptoms appear.

The third phase of syphilis may or may not happen after a certain period of time. For many people, this third phase never comes, while for others it may come very quickly. In the third phase, skin and bone tissues as well as the central nervous system are attacked and destroyed, which may cause severe damage to organ systems and death.

The first two stages of syphilis may be treated with penicillin, but the third stage cannot, which is why it is important to diagnose and treat syphilis in time so as to avoid serious repercussions and even death. The use of condoms will help stop the spread of syphilis like any other STD, but the fact that it also spreads by kissing is a big problem with this disease. This is why you should be very careful engaging in sexual contact with anyone exhibiting symptoms that resemble those of syphilis.

AIDS

Caused by the HIV (Human Immunodeficiency Virus), AIDS (Acquired Immunodeficiency Syndrome) is the most dangerous and yet very widespread disease in the modern world. Unlike herpes or Chlamydia, which are unpleasant and often somewhat dangerous, AIDS is **DEADLY**. This is not an understatement either, as AIDS cannot be cured, cannot be vaccinated against and once you have the disease, it will kill you.

While it is not as common as herpes, HIV infects over 15 million people worldwide and is the modern scourge in many third world countries. This does not under any circumstances mean that westerners are safe, as two million Americans are also infected with HIV, and many of these will develop into AIDS.

The HIV virus is most commonly spread through sex, often anal, but can also be spread through the use of contaminated needles, blood transfusion or transmitted from a mother to her fetus. While the western world was first introduced to HIV by a number of homosexual men being infected, this is by no means a homosexual disease. In Africa where the disease is most widespread, most of the infected are actually heterosexual men and women.

There are two strains of the HIV virus, HIV-1, and HIV-2. While HIV-1 is more common in the western world, HIV-2 is more common in Africa, from where the disease first came. In order to know if you are infected with AIDS, you can see a doctor and do a blood test which will look for HIV antibodies in your blood which only appear in people infected with the virus. This test only produces accurate results about two months after the initial infection, as the antibodies take the time to appear and the first two months are when an infected person is the most contagious. This is why always using condoms is a good idea no matter what, as you can never be safe enough and it is literally impossible to tell with 100% certainty if anyone is infected with HIV.

Once a person is infected with HIV, the virus will begin to slowly destroy their lymphocytes. Lymphocytes are the blood cells which combat infections, and while HIV antibodies will begin to appear in your blood, no one's immune system is strong enough to combat HIV alone. Initially, a person may experience fevers and other symptoms which can be related to any number of diseases. These will go away relatively quickly, and a person will never know they are infected unless they get tested. A period then ensues, often lasting many years, during which no symptoms are exhibited, and nothing of significance happens.

In the meantime, your body continues to combat HIV, but in most cases, the combat is lost after a number of years and the immune system gets damaged to a degree that it can no longer combat some common infections like pneumonia. At this point, a person becomes very sick, and as the immune system is not strong enough to combat this otherwise slight infection, the result is usually death. While the symptoms and infections caused by AIDS can be fought and the person's life prolonged, there is really no way of removing the virus and restoring the immune system, which means death is unavoidable sooner or later. In the western world where advanced medicine is available, an average person infected with HIV can live another 12 years after first being infected.

The HIV virus is so deadly because there is no vaccine and no cure for it yet. This means your only chance of combating HIV is to never contract it in the first place. This is best done by avoiding any potentially dangerous partners and using condoms during every sexual encounter, no matter what you may think of your partner and how sure you may think you are they are not infected. This is a matter of life and death and not one to be taken lightly under any circumstances.

So What Do I Do?

Combatting STDs in the 21st century can be difficult, especially for young people. We live in an age where sex is often practiced for entertainment only and while there is nothing inherently wrong with this, the practice does dramatically increase the chances of contracting STDs.

There is no such thing as safe sex. Sex cannot be safe no matter how much care you take. Just like every time you are put under the influence of anesthesia there is a chance of things going wrong, every time you have sex, there is a chance of contracting an STD. While having a monogamous relationship with someone who has no STDs is a great idea, the fact is, either partner can slip up and contract an STD elsewhere, thus infecting both partners.

Having a relationship before you have sex is a good idea. For starters, very often people who jump into bed on a whim will be those who do it often and such people are very prone to already having STDs, at least the minor ones. Having a relationship before having sex will allow you to get to know the person to some degree and possibly talk about the dangers of STDs.

Using condoms is of course the next step in practicing safe sex, but condoms can break and they are not a foolproof method of protecting against STDs. Still, you should use a condom every single time even if you think they are a hindrance to sexual arousal and enjoyment. While sex without a condom may be a bit more pleasurable, it is also infinitely more dangerous.

If you are someone who already has an STD, it is extremely important to be open about it and talk to any potential sexual partners. While this may be inconvenient, it is the right thing to do, and it is what you would want your partner to do for you and it is crucial to share this kind of information. Once things are as safe as they can be, enjoy having some incredible sex.

Impotence and Premature Ejaculation

While not exactly STDs, impotence and premature ejaculation are two issues that men often experience and can both absolutely ruin sex for you. This is why you will want to recognize and treat these issues to improve your sexual life.

Impotence is the greater of the two evils in this sense, as it entails any kind of condition that prevents a male from getting an erection, which in turn leads to him being unable to perform sexually. There can be various psychological and physical causes for impotence with the most common being old age. Younger men can suffer from impotence as well, however, and in younger men impotence will be a real problem.

The big problem with impotence is that it usually comes gradually. Young people have erections all the time and don't think twice about it. As time goes by, erections become less frequent, and usually it is not even noticeable at all. After some time though, you may find yourself unable to sustain or even get erections, even when you actually need them.

Problems with achieving erections can lead to serious problems in your relationship or marriage and as you notice that erections have become less frequent, you should start seeking help. Instead, many men simply avoid sex and this is neither the right answer nor a solution at all.

There are of course things you could be doing to help yourself. For starters, you may want to try having sex in the morning instead of night. The male sex hormone testosterone is at its peak in the morning and you will also be well-rested, making it easier to get an erection. Try morning sex if you are having trouble maintaining an erection later in the day. Another way of going about things is to insert your non-erect penis into your partner's vagina. The extra stimulation that comes from this may cause your penis to become erect.

When all self-initiated techniques fail, it is time to visit a urologist. Despite what many men think, impotence is usually not permanent and your doctor may be able to help you in many ways. The problem with impotence is usually not physical in nature and sometimes all it takes is your urologist to tell you things are fine for you to get back the confidence you are lacking to perform in bed.

More often than not, aging men simply feel less attractive than they used to, leading to issues with confidence and thus an inability to get an erection. The fear of being unable to perform or please your partner can be very real and can lead to the physical manifestation of the inability to get an erection. To avoid this, a man needs to rebuild his confidence. Working on yourself in other ways, such as working out and dressing up, can help with confidence and reverse the psychologically caused impotence.

If the problem with impotence is a physical one, you may require actual surgery or other kinds of medical help. This includes hydraulic or non-hydraulic implants which either keep the penis in a constant state of mild erection or allow the man to pump the penis up when needed. Injections which relax the penis muscles also exist, allowing better blood flow and easier erections.

The other common issue men face during sex is the exact opposite of impotence and it is the phenomenon of premature ejaculation. While impotent men cannot perform at all, men who experience premature ejaculation finish too fast, making the sexual experience short, less enjoyable and simply anti-climactic.

When having sexual intercourse, it will be crucial for the woman that her man can hold off from ejaculating too fast, as the intercourse has to come to a halt when a man ejaculates, at least for a short (and sometimes for a longer) period. This is why a man needs to train himself to be able to stop from ejaculating prematurely so as to provide the woman with the necessary time for her to enjoy the pleasure of sex.

There is no specific length sexual intercourse should last. Some women can have their orgasm within minutes of penetration, while others will never experience orgasms from intercourse, and a man should adapt to the woman in this regard. If the woman takes about 15 minutes to have an orgasm, you will want to give her at least that long. If she cannot orgasm from intercourse at all, there is nothing wrong with finishing in ten minutes, but the main point is that a man should be able to control his ejaculation and not leave it up to chance.

Some factors such as circumcision or a person's age may influence or cause premature ejaculation. That said, premature ejaculation is more often than not a mental, not a physical issue, as most men are physically capable of lasting quite a bit and it is the mindset that will often control the ejaculation.

If you do have a problem with finishing too fast during intercourse, or even having an orgasm before the intercourse has even began, there are many techniques you can use to stop this from happening.

For starters, thinking about something else during intercourse is something that can work really well. While in an optimal scenario you will want to give yourself completely to your partner and really be in the moment, your partner is not likely to notice if you briefly switch your thoughts from her to something completely mundane and simply continue having the intercourse mechanically for a while. This method will likely remove the sensation that builds up and stop you from ejaculating before you want to.

There are other things you can do as well to prevent premature ejaculation, and especially for young men, masturbating before having a sexual act can greatly diminish the chances of premature ejaculation. The male libido is strong in youth and very often young men can ejaculate many times in one day, so you may want to masturbate before having sex, to make sure you can perform long enough.

Using condoms when having sex is highly recommended either way, as you will want to protect yourself from STDs, but as an added bonus, people who experience premature ejaculation will usually last longer when wearing a condom than when not wearing one.

Chapter 14 –

Sex and Culture

Different cultures have different attitudes towards sex. Americans and Europeans tend to be more open about sex and their desires whereas other cultures can be a lot more private. Asian culture typically has the woman as being very submissive and meek, allowing the man to do with her as he pleases. These couples are generally known to not allow others in the bedroom with them. Sex is simply done between husband and wife. A lot of American men find Asian women desirable because of their known submissive qualities in the bedroom. This culture also frowns upon the woman engaging with other men without the husband's approval.

Hispanic culture generally practices sex as a means for reproduction due to their strong Catholic beliefs against birth control. Due to the lack of birth control, Hispanic families tend to have larger than average families. Hispanic men are generally the workers in the family while the woman stays at home and cares for the kids.

American and European culture is a melting pot of desires. Because there are so many different types of people in these regions, there is a huge mix of what people find arousing and desirable. You may have clashing cultural beliefs on sex that give rise to new and exciting techniques. These cultures, in some cases, welcome the idea of bringing in other couples into the bedroom for fun, known as "swinging." These cultures also have resorts and clubs focused on nudity and sexual expression. Porn is common and in some ways, encouraged among men and women equally.

Sex culture has also changed throughout the centuries and even most recently, the decades. In the early 19th century, sex was between a husband and wife and was talked much about outside of the bedroom. Earlier than that, men were permitted to have more than one wife. As time went on, the "roaring twenties" brought about a whole new type of sexuality with the introduction of the flapper.

The depression hit, wars were fought and at the end of it all, there was a giant baby boom from all the soldiers that had come back from the war. As time continually passed, the joining or a husband and wife was seen as traditional and was something to aspire to. Men and women had sex with their husbands and wives and that was that, not much else to elaborate on. The early twentieth century began to glamorize sexuality more in music, style and movies.

Today, there are many cultures that only practice sex as a means for reproduction. There are certain practices we Americans may find to be taboo, but for other cultures, these are the norms and what Americans do is a form of taboo. Americans are one of the cultures that practices sex as a means for pleasure more often than for reproduction purposes.

In the current day and age, sex and sexuality is a topic that is no longer kept under wraps. Although the traditional, husband and wife sex is practiced, it is not uncommon for couples to be more adventurous and invite more people into the bedroom if it's a mutual agreement. There is also more use of sex toys, pornography, lingerie and bondage than previous decades combined. In past, present and future times, sex provides pleasure for all cultures alike, in combination with a natural desire to reproduce.

Cultural Taboo

There are a lot of different practices and arousals throughout the world that may seem like taboo to us. When trying to gain a perspective on how certain activities like this are accepted, you have to realize that this is all they have ever known. In most cases, they are born into the culture and never know anything but their own. In some cases, the culture they are in could view our traditional sexual practices as taboo.

Sex dolls have come a long way since they were first invented. These dolls are now sold and can make sounds and short movements to give a more realistic feel. Some people will buy these dolls and treat them as their significant other. It can seem strange to some to house a doll in your home as a person, this is why it is considered "taboo." However, the people who engage in this see this as normal and enjoyable.

There is a tribe deep within Central India that participates in a ceremony called Ghotul. This ceremony consists of teenage men and women celebrating and participating in orgies and sexual romps. There are also teachings of songs, culture and food. The teenage girls drink a natural liquid to reduce the likelihood of pregnancy, and every night the girl picks a new sexual partner. If one of the girls does become pregnant, the whole tribe adopts the baby because the father is unknown.

In the Himalayas, there is a culture that involves having one wife for a group of brothers. Due to the high poverty rate and low amounts of land for agriculture, wives generally give birth to multiple children to help work on the farm and make money. When the sons get older, a single wife is found for the group of brothers and is shared among them, so that way the fathers land does not have to be split between his many sons. The wife has to then make a sexual schedule so that each man can have his time with her to avoid any jealousy or feelings of negligence.

In Papua New Guinea, children begin having sex as young as age 6.

Girls usually begin sexual activities between ages 6-8 whereas the boys generally start between 10 and 12. It is accepted and encouraged to begin having sexual intercourse at a young age. There are also no stigmas against having premarital sex, as it is commonly practiced within the culture.

Chapter 15 -
Sex Through the Ages

Sex has always been an important part of the human experience. Like other species, humans use sex to procreate, making it an inevitable part of our lives. It has been so ever since the most ancient of times and all the cultures in the world have had their distinctive way of viewing sex. If we look over the entire earth and through all the ages, we will come across diverse approaches, from those perfectly liberal and open to sex of all kinds to the most closed and limited sexual cultures possible.

It is well-known that some eras in human history, such as the Ancient Greek period, were marked by sex, making it an important part of their culture and praising it in every sense. The medieval European period or the culture of the Muslim countries limited sex to a strictly marital activity not to be spoken of in public forums.

We will take a closer look at the way sex has impacted various cultures and lands through the ages and find out what similarities and diversities were present in lands from east to west.

China

Since ancient times, China has been a very sexist society where men enjoyed much more sexual freedoms than women. A woman's virginity was considered her greatest value and virtue and was to be kept safe at all costs. Men, on the other hand, had pretty much every right to have sex with whomever they pleased without any real punishment.

For women, sex was reserved for marriage. Men had the option of marrying one woman but were also allowed to find other women for sexual pleasure and name them their concubines. Slaves in a man's possession were also available for sex, which meant rich men would often have many sexual partners at once while a woman was restricted to her husband, who was usually chosen by her family.

Not only was sexuality allowed for men, but ancient Chinese art has greatly propagated it. Many works of Chinese literature describe all sorts of marital and extramarital sexual activities, many of which include homosexuality and bestiality. Nevertheless, Chinese culture never openly adopted any of these practices and has always remained very patriarchal, and has tried to claim that Chinese men and women remain pure until marriage and exercise fidelity once married.

The patriarchal bonds that once kept the country so restricted have been somewhat lifted in recent decades with more and more people jumping into premarital sexual intercourse without any intent of marriage, and homosexuality becoming a somewhat accepted phenomenon. Still, the tight grip of the Chinese government makes things extremely difficult for homosexuals and women who openly exercise premarital sex, and they are often stigmatized for their behavior by the conservative Chinese society.

Japan

Like China, Japan has had a long tradition of women being put in second place when it comes to sex. Most women were expected to find a suitable husband, get married, perform household duties and be at their man's disposal for sex. Men, on the other hand, were allowed to seek sexual comfort outside of the family with any woman of their choosing, prostitute or otherwise.

An interesting and somewhat unique practice that stems from Japan is the existence of Geishas. Geishas were ladies who were trained in many fine arts and crafts such as music, dance, and intellectual endeavors. Their primary role was not to satisfy men sexually, as this was not their duty, but rather provide them female companionship at an intellectual level. Their beauty and education allowed them to capture men's minds, but they were able to choose whether to have intercourse with a customer or not. Sex or no sex, geishas were paid exceptionally well and were considered a great luxury.

Geishas aside, Japan is a place where many sexual fetishes are quite present among the population, yet sex is often regarded as a taboo topic. Like in most Asian cultures, fathers do their best to keep their daughters safe from sex until they are married, while men are free to run rampant and have sex whenever it is available.

Practices such as sexual fetishes and homosexuality were hidden away in Japanese society for many centuries, despite being quite accepted in early Japan. In recent decades, the Japanese have rediscovered many of these and homosexuality is not exactly frowned upon in Japan as it is in China.

India

As Indian religions and morals are for the most part much more liberal than many of the western ones, sex was much less of a taboo through the history of India than in other countries.

Many ancient Indian texts refer to sexual activities, with the most famous of these texts being the well-known Kama Sutra, a literal guide to sex which was first designed to help Indian people satisfy their marital partners sexually. In India, sex was a duty for both the husband and the wife and was to be indulged in but kept as a private matter between the married couple.

With the exception of the ruling classes, most people lived monogamous lives, but sex was not frowned upon. Certain western influences made the approach to sex in India somewhat more conservative in the later centuries, but the latest trend has been a rebirth of sexual liberalism in India.

The famous tantric sex also stems from India. The tantric sexual methods became known to westerners, and have become widely spread in recent decades and have captured the imagination of many. Tantric sex is said to be a much more fulfilling and complete sexual experience than normal sex but for many Indians, it is considered a path to complete enlightenment rather than a means of corporal pleasure.

The two schools of thought in India always saw sex as either an absolute duty of marital partners to one another or a hindrance to enlightenment which is to be absolutely avoided. As such, there was always some tension between these groups, but India, in general, was historically one of the more sexually liberal countries in Asia.

Greece

Of all the ancient cultures, Greek culture had one of the most open and liberal approaches to sex. From religion to literature and art, sex was considered a normal and important part of human lives. Men enjoyed sex with their wives as well as with prostitutes and other women. Also, men would often engage in sex with much younger women and even boys, as every form of sex including homosexuality and bisexuality was both accepted and encouraged.

In ancient Greece, you could say that anything was normal, as people quite liberally enjoyed homosexual relations, had sex with much younger women. Even rape was an accepted part of the culture, both during the war as an act of dominance and during peacetime when some forms of rape were an accepted social construct.

Even the Greek religion endorsed sexuality greatly, with the gods themselves often being extremely promiscuous and enjoying all forms of sexual and other carnal pleasures. Greek religious temples held within them elite prostitutes who charged higher prices and were considered a special kind of luxury. In either case, Greek people enjoyed their sexuality to the fullest and did not have much shame, which can be seen in their art even to this day.

Rome

Like most other ancient cultures, Roman culture was fairly sexist and male-oriented. In ancient Rome, a woman was allowed to have sexual intercourse with her husband only, while men had every right to seek sexual companionship from slaves, prostitutes and lower-class women in general.

The Roman law included punishments for rape and adultery, but a man was only seen as committing adultery if he would have relations with a married woman. Otherwise it was not punishable.

Both heterosexual and homosexual relations were celebrated in ancient Rome and very much indulged in. Roman males and females both took good care of their bodies, and athletic looks were a sign of masculinity.

Roman culture did not look down on a man having homosexual relations if he was the one with the dominating role. In fact, they did not even make a distinction between the two. As long as a man was dominant, he was perceived as manly. Sexual relations with prostitutes were a part of everyday life in Rome and prostitution was legal and practiced very openly in city streets and squares.

Much of the Roman art and philosophy also included sexual motives, as various drawings, paintings and books were made using such motives. For instance, The Art of Love by the poet Ovid was a series of instructional poems that were meant to teach men and women how to attract the opposite sex. Many other books and myths included sexual topics such as adultery, incest, rape, and others.

Middle Ages Europe

Sexuality in the middle ages was largely regulated and basically forbidden in most cases by the church, whose grasp over Europe in this period was extremely tight. According to the church, no sex was to take place unless the two partners were married, and even, in that case, there were literally dozens of rules that had to be obeyed and followed to make the sexual act "pure."

According to the church, sex was not meant to be used for pleasure, but rather only for procreation. Women were obligated to have relations with their husbands for procreation and also pleasure, but within very confined limitations. These limitations meant that oral sex, anal sex, any type of a fetish, getting fully naked and even what we would today call "making out" were completely out of the picture. As you can imagine, this made sex a lot less appealing and satisfactory for both parties.

Furthermore, sex was also forbidden in many occasions for husbands and wives. For instance, having sex before nightfall was considered a sin and doing it on a Sunday was a sin as well, as that was the Lord's Day. Having sex on Thursday or Friday wasn't recommended either as those were the days of preparation for the communion. The times of Lent, Pentecost and Christmas preparation were also to be periods of abstinence. Combined, these three made up for more than 130 days per year. Add to that the Sundays, Thursdays and Fridays as well as high holidays and it is safe to say those who followed these rules didn't really have much sex at all.

For those people who did commit these various "sins," there were various types of punishment and penance that were to be used to make one pure again. Some of the laws would see young boys whipped by their parents for masturbating and an adult man would have to abstain from eating meat for days in order to make penance.

While these laws did exist, many people did not take them too seriously and went behind the church's back to have sexual relations either way. This meant a lot of hiding had to happen and ironically, the church buildings were often used to have sex as they were usually the most secluded and private places in medieval towns and villages.

Prostitution was another act that was frowned upon by the official church authorities, but urban centers of Europe very much allowed prostitution as they deemed it to be a necessary evil. As such, you could find a brothel in every major city in Europe, and they were well-regulated as well.

It is safe to say that the Middle Ages were somewhat of a dark period for sexuality in Europe as the overall culture was less than liberal and you could get punished for most sexual acts, which made people more reluctant to engage in them. It was not until the period of Renaissance that a new sexual revolution would sweep Europe and bring back much of the ancient practices.

Modern Day Sexuality

Today, most of the western world has embraced sexuality as something normal and to some degree have possibly even perverted it into a degenerated state. Today, sex is everywhere around us, from the oversexualized music and movies to actual pornography and things like sex toys being sold out in the open. The modern day western society quite clearly embraces sex as a major part of its culture.

Homosexuality is becoming an accepted practice in much of the world, with more and more countries allowing same-sex marriages and child adoption. This very progressive way of looking at things has stirred much debate among religious and various other moralist groups, but sex is here to stay, and it seems now more than ever society is leaning towards a very liberal approach to human sexuality.

Even the eastern societies that used to be very closed-minded when it came to sex and the topic itself was a taboo such as China are becoming more and more open to accepting homosexuality and human sexuality in general as a normal phenomenon. The only places with a significant number of residents that still remain exceptionally closed when it comes to sexuality are the Islamic countries where many sexual "offenses" are still punishable by death to this day. These atrocious practices may be a sign that the human race has not yet evolved to a truly liberal state, but significant progress has certainly been made and the global combat to free people's minds continues.

Chapter 16 –
Sex Party Scenes

Orgies couples/ singles

If you are new to the world of sex parties and orgies, then I am sure you have some level of curiosity. You might be wondering what it actually feels like to be part of an orgy or be in a room where multiple people are shagging one another.

If you wish to be part of an orgy, then you have to know a few things in advance that are as follows.

To start with, it is important to follow a code of conduct at such parties. You should not be rude or pushy. If there are only a few girls and a lot of boys then they have to patiently wait for their turn. You might not be invited back if you are rude or pushy.

There might be a lot of people coming from different parts of the world and a mixture of both genders. Most of these parties usually happen post dinner and when people are mostly intoxicated. You might end up getting bodily fluids from both sexes and must be prepared to be in close contact with people belonging to your gender.

It is important to be respectful of others and respect their choices. If they happen to say no to someone then you have to respect them and back off. Others have to do the same with you if they are asked to back off.

There can be some orgies where people meet up beforehand to get to know each other a little better. They might announce a meet up at a restaurant or a bar and doing so can help newcomers familiarize themselves with those involved. It can help them stay calm.

Some people might be in costume and masks. This might not mean they are being anonymous. It simply means they are engaging in role-play.

Swinger clubs

Just like orgies, you have to know a few things about swinger clubs. I am sure you have thought of being a part of a swinger club but never really knew what to expect. Well, here are some things that you need to know.

- The very first thing to understand is that both you and your partner have to be on the same page. Before you take your partner to a swinger's party, tell them about it and explain that you and he/she are going to engage in sexual activity. Even if you have discussed it with them and have their consent, you have to inform them about it before entering a swinger's party.

- Once you decide to start swinging with your partner, you have to make a few rules to stick to. It is best for both partners to decide on a few rules to follow before entering such parties. Some of them include basics like kissing is allowed but not oral sex. You can change the rules when you think it is the right time to do so.

- It will be a good idea to experiment a little. Start out with a high-end party or a club where group sex is common. Be a regular at the parties so that you get to know the people involved. It will be more comfortable for you compared to any online groups where you don't know people.

- It is important to be social at such events. Do not stick to people you are comfortable with. Experiment with new people and expand your social circle. Walk up to people you like and say hi to them. Be friendly and talk to everybody at the function.

- It is advisable to get to the party early. Start drinking when every one else starts. If you are sober and they are drunk then it can be uncomfortable for you. Show up on time and chat up the hosts and the people at the party. Get comfortable with the bar tenders.

Engage in conversation with your partner and decide on a point in time when both of you wish to start getting physical with each other.

- It is important to know some of the words that are used at such parties. Knowing them can help you remain comfortable at parties. Hard swap refers to couples that are interested in fully exchanging their partners sexually. A unicorn refers to a woman who goes to swinger events alone. A soft swap refers to couples that are interested in exchanging partners but will not go all the way with them. Swingers like to refer to their way of living as a "lifestyle."

- It is essential not to overdo the alcohol. It might end up affecting your overall experience. You will be extremely excited at such an event no doubt but overdoing the alcohol can end up making you feel sleepy or tired and you might not be able to perform. You might also end up being aggressive.

- As a rule, try to set only realistic expectations and do not go for a hard swap right from the beginning. It might end up intimidating you. Go for a soft swap first and make sure you and your partner are both comfortable with it. These parties usually start late at night so be prepared for some late night action. Do not get bored by going too early and thinking nobody is going to swing.

- It is best to allow the woman to lead the way. Allow your lady to set the rules and decide what she is comfortable with. Don't be pushy and get her to do things she might not want to do. You must allow her to do what she would like to do at the party and let her call the shots.

- As much as you think you know what a swinger party is going to be like based on what you have heard and watched on the Internet, it would be best to attend a party first to know what actually goes on and then decide whether you want to be a part of it. You might find it quite intimidating at first but it will be fine once you get the hang of it.

- Have a talk about your experience with your partner and

consider reworking the rules every four months or so. You might not be comfortable with some things and decide to not engage in them at the next party. Similarly, you might want to start adding new things that you would like to try out at the next party.

Remember that communication is key and you and your partner have to communicate with each other so that there will not be any tiffs and the two of you can have a great experience.

Cuckolds and Cukcakes

Before we get started with these topics, you must first familiarize yourself with these words.

A cuckold refers to a man who enjoys watching his wife having sex with another man.

Cukcakes refers to a subset of cuckolding where two of the participants will be women. Usually, cuckolding will involve the man being submissive - known as the bull - who has sex with the female partner in front of another man who happens to be the cuckold and a submissive partner. The cuckold will be helpless and will only watch his wife being pleased by another man. The situation is referred to as cuckqueaning and the female bull is known as the cuckcake. The cuckquean will have to watch the cuckcake have sex with the submissive partner who can either be male or female.

A female cuckold refers to a submissive woman who gets masochistic pleasure by seeing her partner having sex with someone. This pleasure mostly comes from humiliation and the mental unrest that can prevail from knowing that your partner is being pleased by someone else or that they are having more fun with someone else. It is believed that these cucks idealize humiliation as a way to seek pleasure.

Cuckolding is not the same as singing or having threesomes. The cuckold will not participate in these parties. The cuckold and his partner have to have an emotional bonding of some sort as otherwise there will not be humiliation. Most of the cuckqueans will be married women. A difference that exists between cuckolds and cuckqueens is that they will both focus on the woman that her partner is having sex with.

This concept is now quite common as many partners are turned on by the idea of their partners having sex with others. Most couples talk about it all the time and might start out by watching threesome porn. In most of these, two people will be having sex while the third will be watching. The two men might not necessarily interact at all as the cuckold or husband is only there to watch the couple have sex and not participate in the session. The husband is referred to as the cuck and the other guy is a bull or stud. The woman is referred to as the hot wife.

Although humiliation is a theme, it might not always be a part of the show. Some people like to involve it as a part of the activity in order to derive greater pleasure but there can be some who will be a part of it without incorporating humiliation. Some look at such events as a way to be humiliated or made to feel shameful about themselves.

This concept works on the principle of jealousy. It is believed that most humans are jealous when they see their partner enjoying sex with someone else. This experience can make the partner look a lot more attractive. It can make the cuckold feel like the partner is much hotter than she is and he will consequently be more attracted to her. It is better known as sperm competition where the person will feel like he is competing with someone else for his partner. The aspect of humiliation has to do with breaking taboos.

Getting started with it

Before you get started with this, you and your partner will have to understand certain aspects of cuckolding. Have a talk with your husband and find out what he considers to be humiliation. In most cases, cuckolds like to be compared to bulls in humiliating ways. The bull might be more muscular or taller or better looking or a lot more masculine etc. He might have a better sex drive and a stronger stamina. Most cucks will be turned on if the bulls have bigger cocks that can satisfy their hot wives in ways that they cannot.

These are regular ideologies and your husband might have some different ideas. Some like buying sexy lingerie for their hot wives that they will only be using for the bulls and not for them.

So, start off by asking him things like "What does humiliation mean to you? What would be your dream scenario?" "How and when do you want me to do it? As my bull and I are having sex? When it's just you and I? Outside of the bedroom?" "Will there be some off-limit things"

Sometime, it is a good idea to start off by exploring humiliation between yourselves. There might be ways in which you can shame him yourself. It can help to explore some of the boundaries that you would like to set during cuckqueaning. It might also help you avoid any complications arising out of involving a third person if it is just the two of you.

You can come up with domination and submission games that are designed to lead to humiliation. Simply telling your husband your fantasies about the bull of your dreams can make him jealous.

If you wish to get started with a real bull then it will be important to find the ideal bull. The Internet can be a good source to find one. Cuckolding and humiliation might be tough to explain to someone new. So, it would be a good idea to find someone who is aware of the concepts and has been in such situations before. Many sites such as adult friend finder and cuckold finder can be used to find such cuckolds.

Make sure you clearly mention what you and your husband are

looking for. Allow your husband to express his desires and what he would expect of a bull.

There might be cuckold specific sex parties in your area that you can visit. Again, the Internet can help you find them.

Doms and subs

Doms and subs refer to people who play the role of a dominant partner in a sexual setting and the other plays a submissive role. There are no rules as to who can be the Dom and who can be the sub. In some cases, the woman might be the Dom and in some the man.

Doms will be dominant right from the beginning and can command the subs to do things to their liking. They can command their partner to disrobe or wear things that they fancy. Some doms like to collar their subs with a leash. They might also have leg cuffs or chains or spreader bars.

If you will be going to a dom-sub party, then prepare for humiliation if you happen to be the sub. In most parties, the Dom will present the Sub and explain features including pussy, breasts and ass and might use hands to smack them or penetrate. Breasts can be pinched and pressed in order to make the Sub cry out for help. If the Sub happens to be a male then their cocks will be grabbed and pulled. Their balls will be played with and can make the Sub yelp. Male doms like subs to parade around the party with their cocks in the sub's hands.

The subs eyes are usually looking down and their heads are bent down as well. The doms will be looking at the sub's assets, which happens to be their main area of interest. The subs are expected to fulfill the doms sexual desires and not be distracted by anything else that is around them. Most of the subs are trained that way.

If you happen to be at a swinger party with your partner then you have to decide before hand who will be playing what role. Again, it will be best for the lady to decide what role her husband is allowed to play. If you are swinging with an experienced couple then it would be better to let them take the lead. Sometimes it might be difficult to figure out what certain couples want. You have to give it some time so that you can understand what they are looking for and whether you are interested in participating. You will have to understand that once you decide to be someone's sub, you will have to do as they wish.

The use of toys is a big part of doms and Sub parties. Right from dildos to anal gems to other sexual toys, doms will use them to treat subs how they wish to treat them. Doms will try to get a reaction from their subs by subjecting them to humiliation.

In a party, there will be many subs each one told to do as their doms say. Doms can tell subs to lie down and spread their legs for masturbation or get them in a position of their choice. Some might be asked to go down on each other. Some will be asked to poke sex toys into the other's orifices. Some subs can be made to kneel down and made to act as a table for drinks. Some subs can be treated as waitresses and made to bring drinks out for the doms.

These doms and subs can be straight, lesbians or gays. Sometimes, lesbian doms can make their lesbian subs be pleasured by male subs and vice versa. As long as the parties involved do not mind, they are allowed to engage in any activity of their choice.

In a typical scenario, male doms will get their subs to suck on their fingers. They are trained to take command and do as their doms tell them to. They might also be trained to suck in a certain erotic way. Some like to listen to what the crowd wants and do as they want. The crowds mostly do not get involved and only get the doms and subs to act like they would want them to. But some doms might get the crowd involved and make the Sub please some people from the crowd.

Dirty talk forms a big part of the show or party. Both the doms and

Sub engage in dirty talk. The crowd too can get involved and talk dirty while the activity is taking place.

Most of the doms and Sub parties will have sweatboxes. These are better known as BDSM dungeons and will consist of all the equipment needed to carry out the BDSM activities. There can be boards hung from the ceiling with metal loops and a strong metal strap that will be used to cuff the wrists of the sub. There might be X braces that can be used to punish the subs and also chains and braces along with spread bars, whips, braids, tails etc.

By now you must have understood what a Dom and Sub relationship is all about. It does not always have to be about power play and can sometimes be a way to spruce up a couple's sex life.

The roles need not be predefined and the couple can decide to switch their roles. This can help to introduce variety into their sex lives and their relationship as a whole. Subs usually take the role of serving the Dom in a way the Dom decides. This can be about serving food or pleasing them or being punished.

A lot of people tend to compare Dom - Sub relationships with traditional vanilla relationships. But there can be a bit more power play involved during the sexual activities. But most vanilla relationships can predefine the roles of the partners. The roles and actions can be a bit explicit in a Dom and Sub relationship.

BDSM is usually seen in bad light or associated with negative thinking. Some might think of it as abuse. But this not true. The actions have to be consensual. There can be some negotiations and certain ground rules that have to be followed. There can be checklists that are exchanged which will mention the various terms and conditions. Role-play will be predefined. It is about being aware and knowing what doms and subs experience.

In order to get started with it with your partner, or get started in general, you have to talk it out with them. Communication will be key so that you can both be on the same page. Define what roles you would like to play out. Do not assume that you partner would like to get into a specific role just because they have a certain personality type. Ask them what they would enjoy being.

Start by making a list of activities belonging to the BDSM community that you are aware of and then mention a yes, no or maybe next to it. Ask your partner to do the same and then match your lists. You might be able to establish common ground. It will be important to only find tasks that both are willing to engage in. Write down fantasies if you have any so that role-play can become easy.

There can be a lot of places where you can look for information about this kind of sex. BDSM websites make for a good place to start. There will be information about this and the kind of practices and relationships that can be played out. There might be some local fetish fairs and some kink events and demonstrations or workshops. You can also refer to books.

Apart from a BDSM relationship, you can also choose to have a vanilla relationship with your partner. This means that you can be normal and engage in normal sexual activities. You do not always have to play out your fetishes. Again, this depends on you and your partner and what you would like to have.

Here are some games that Doms and Subs can engage in.

Dom Worship

One of the most popular games to play with subs is dominating them by catering to them the whole day. The sub's role will be to please the Dom and pay full attention to their needs. This can include giving them a body massage, dressing up the way they want you to dress up, wearing sex toys, performing oral sex on them etc. These are some of the things that subs can do for doms. There can be many other things such as cooking naked, engaging in other sexual behaviors etc. the Sub engages in whatever pleases the dom.

Slave Training

This is a simple and interesting game to play when you are trying to get the feel of the Dom and Sub game. It can also be referred to as a set of rules that the two involved parties abide by. Some of them are as follows.

- The Sub will only obey instructions and do everything that the Dom asks them to do.
- The subs will not do anything apart from what they being asked to do.
- The subs will not speak until they are spoken to.
- Subs will not make any eye contact with the Dom unless they are asked to and so on.

Devotion

If you have not yet decided on boundaries, then start off by talking sexy with your Dom and get them to list out all the fantasies that they have. The Sub is also allowed to have boundaries. He/she too is allowed to make the list. Just the act of discussing these boundaries can prove to be an interesting game.

<u>Deciding punishment</u>

It will be important to predetermine the punishment. Punishment forms a big part of the Dom and Sub relationship. If you have not yet explored this particular aspect of a Dom and Sub relationship then now is a good time to do so. Punishments are usually engaged in to showcase the subs devotion to the Dom. The subs can choose the type of punishment that they would be prepared to receive. It should be ethical and humane and should not hurt the sub. Here are some of the punishments that are quite common in the world of BDSM.

- Spanking using the hand, paddle, belt, whip or any other items.
- Using nipple clamps.
- Taking the Sub to the climax but not being allowed to orgasm.
- Not allowed to have any contact of any sort.
- Making them carry out tasks. These tasks can be sexual in nature or not. For example, it can be something like giving oral sex or cleaning the garden.
- Being called a name the whole day.
- Starting over after getting to the half way mark of a task etc.

Permission game

The permission game is one where the Sub will ask the Dom for permission to perform all the tasks that they want to do. This can be pretty much every single task including going to the bathroom, taking a nap, eating etc. It can also be about asking permission to do things inside the bedroom such as touching the Dom, kissing the Dom, pleasing the Dom etc. The Dom can decide the activities that the Sub has to ask permission for before carrying the action out and can punish the Sub if they do not follow instructions.

Permission to come

This game is pretty much like the previous one except that the Sub asks the Dom permission to come or orgasm. If the Sub happens to have an orgasm without permission then he or she can be punished for it.

Performing tasks

This game involves the Sub performing certain predetermined tasks on a regular basis. The Dom will assign certain tasks that the Sub has to perform every day. This can be spending some time performing oral sex, cleaning the room floor, cooking a meal etc. The Dom can decide this for the sub. The Dom can also determine other rules for the game such as the Sub wearing specific clothing or outfit as decided by the Dom, setting timelines within which the Sub has to finish the chores etc. The Dom will inspect the work from time to time and if it has not been done properly then he/she will punish the sub.

Getting a reward

If the Dom is impressed by the Sub then he/she can offer rewards to them. They can access the rewards if they fulfill certain tasks and chores on time. For example, if the Sub manages to give the Dom an orgasm, then he or she can be rewarded for it.

Conditional Rewards

The above can be further explored by the Dom offering conditional rewards to the sub. This means that the rewards will come with a catch. The subs will only get their rewards if they do the task to the doms liking and can be punished if they do not. Say for example, the Dom offers the Sub a break to engage in an activity of their choice but only if they engage in oral sex for a given period of time.

The Points game

The Points game is one where the chores and rewards are based on a points system. The Dom can assign certain number of points to the tasks and chores that the Sub will be made to carry out. The number of points that the Sub earns can be used to exchange for rewards. The Dom will decide the rewards and the number of points that need to be used. This will make for an interesting game, as the subs will feel more involved in the game. They will also have a say in the rewards that they expect to get from the activities.

Bondage

Bondage is a common practice in Dom and Sub games. In this, the Dom ties down the Sub in some way such as by using ropes or cuffing them. The Dom will control the Sub in all ways. Bondage tape, rope and other such systems can be put in place. The Dom can perform sexual activities on the Sub when they have been held in bondage.

<u>Role-play</u>

Engaging in role-play is a common aspect of Dom and Sub relationships. Playing specific roles can help them let go of their inhibitions and make the relationship more dynamic. Here are some of the roles that the doms and subs can play out.

- King or queen and helper
- Celebrities and personal assistants
- Thief and police
- Detective and criminal
- Kidnapper and victim
- Sailor and pirate
- Client and prostitute

There can be many other roles that the doms and subs can decide upon. <u>Engaging in servitude</u>
Servitude is being available to serve to the Dom at specific times. The Dom will decide on these times based on whatever is convenient to them. These can be tasks outside the bedroom and not always inside. The Dom can choose specific times and dates that will be blocked for the sub. The Sub has to be ready at these times. The Sub should be prepared to be penetrated at the specific times. They can be asked to be quiet until they hear the next command.

<u>Keeping your Sub crawling back for more</u>

It is obvious that all doms want their subs to come back for more. Here are some tips that can help you have just that and more!

Before we look at tips, you must know that domination is not the act itself but more about its application. It happens to be the state of mind of the Dom and not necessarily any specific task that is to be carried out.

Having said that, domination can range from sexual activity to pillow talk to other things that are related to BDSM in general. Remember that some subs like it hard. Their threshold will be higher than others and might be able to tolerate more punishment than regular subs. This is generally not considered as torture as long as the act is consensual.

Before you get started, it is essential to set boundaries. Even if BDSM is all about bondage, doms and subs, there have to be guidelines that have to be followed. Not following them can lead to issues and discrepancies. The idea is to make it enjoyable for both the parties involved and not just the Dom or just the sub.

The Dom should respect it if the Sub is uncomfortable in any way including physically or mentally. When the Sub hands over all control to the Dom, it becomes important for the Dom to exercise caution and ensure that the Sub is made to feel safe at all times. Boundaries must not be disrespected no matter what the situation is. There should not be any scope for experimentation. Remember that the power lies in the hands of the Sub and not the Dom. The Sub decides what is okay and what is not and also has access to the brakes.

It is important to have a list of safe words that can be used to stop ongoing activities. Sometimes the Sub might not be able to come up with the right words. You have to make sure that you read their sign language and understand that they are in discomfort. If they seem hesitant and feel intimidated, then stop and talk to them about it. See if you can continue or it is best to wrap up the session. As soon as the Sub uses the safe word, the session has to be ended. You can free them if they are ties and make them comfortable. Discuss with them what might have gone wrong. Just because they are fine again does not mean you continue as the safe word means it is time to stop the activities. Look at it as a learning experience.

Be considerate and kind to your sub. This is an important point that needs to be stressed. There will always be some things off the list even if you are being aggressive with your partner.

Passion

It will be essential to be passionate with your partner. Show them how much you love having sex with them. Kiss them while grabbing their face. Grope them and say things like "this is mine now." Pin them against the wall or push them on the bed and control their movement. If they happen to like something, then play along and give them what they want.

Be open

It will be important to be open to your partner at all times. This means that you remain eager to do what you want with them. You must not feel intimidated or shy. Go for what you think is right and follow your instincts. Communicate openly with them. Tell that about a certain part of their body that appeals the most to you.

Guessing

Keep them guessing. Do things they are not expecting. The more surprises you give them, the more shock value will be attached to it. Keep up with it and do not let them catch a breath. Spank them, rub them and make them feel good. Use your mouth everywhere on them. Be it licking them or sucking or biting, give them one surprise after another.

Control orgasm

It will be a good way to please your partner by controlling their orgasm. It can serve as a tool to tease them and can be used as a means to make them come back for more. Take them to the point where they beg you to let them orgasm. When you finally do let them do it, it will be extremely satisfying for them and they will love the experience. It will be like you are telling your partner when the right time arrives to climax. You will also be able to time it with their climax.

Two-way street

You, the Dom, have to allow your Sub to please you just as much as you please them. Do not make it a one-way street where only you please them. They should be given the chance to please you and you must do things that satisfy you. You are allowed to give them instructions and tell them what you are after. Talk to them constantly and make sure they do exactly what it is that you are looking to get.

Gagging

Gagging is a common aspect of BDSM and one that is favored by many enthusiasts. Gagging is done to control the way in which they communicate with you. It puts them at your mercy. Bondage is used as a tool to take claim of their body, but make sure they are comfortable and able to communicate with you.

Sexy words

Use sexy words while engaging in the act as compare to derogatory ones. They are more likely to be turned on by words such as beautiful and sexy as compared to slut or bitch.

Use words that they would like to hear from you. You can ask them to tell you such words that they like being called and say them out loud every time you engage in the act.

Mark territory

Use your cum as a way to mark your territory. Tell them in advance where you will be coming on them so that they are prepared for it. Once you cum on a certain area of their body, tell that that the area now belongs to you.

Toys

The use of tools and toys is a very vast subject. There are many toys and different ways in which each one can be used. You do not have to buy anything special and can make do with things that are already present in your home such as kitchen ladles to spank, ropes, blindfolds, belts, gags etc. taking full control over your partner can help you have an enjoyable experience.

Aftercare

Remember that aftercare is extremely important. Once you have finished, cuddle with them and tell them how much you enjoy being with them. Offer them something to drink and calm them. Get their feedback on the session and ask them about the things they enjoyed and the things they did not.

Queen of spades tattoo on a female

The queen of spades tattoo is used by women to signal that they are only interested in black cocks. They can get a permanent or temporary tattoo on them and it will mostly be hidden. It means that they are specifically looking for sex with black men. It is seen as a powerful tattoo that signals to men that women too can have sexual preferences and are not there just to please men. Women can have this tattoo or wear a piece of clothing or have a pendant on them with this symbol. They all indicate that she loves or craves black cocks.

If a hot wife has this tattoo on her then it means that she is craving a black bull. A branded queen of spades tattoo where a Q is present inside the spade stands for the woman's lifelong commitment to black men.

Women usually hide this tattoo on a daily basis and will only put it on show during parties.

Chapter 17 –
Sex Toys; Types of Toys for Him/Her

Furniture

Sex furniture can range from simple cushions to complicated contraptions. It is always a good idea to buy available sex furniture as compared to making them, as you might not be able to come up with an effective design. But if you happen to be DIY savvy then you can go for it.

Here is some information on sex furniture.

- It is a piece of furniture that helps with sexual experience.
- It is mostly used to introduce excitement and aid with getting into certain positions that might be difficult without the help of furniture.

Types of sex furniture

There are many types of sex furniture and they are as follows.

Wedges

These refer to triangular pieces of foam that are used to support the body if you wish to maintain a certain position for longer periods of time. These are flexible pieces and can be used for non-sexual poses as well. They are available in different sizes and you can choose whatever size suits your needs. There will be advanced and beginner's models available.

Beds

These beds are not regular beds that one will find in their bedrooms.

They are custom ones that can be inflated or deflated and that have restraints attached to them. You can add sheets and pillows that can give you extra sensations during sex and they can also be cleaned up easily.

Chairs

There are many types of chairs that can be used to enhance sexual experiences. Some of them are as follows.

Queening chairs refer to low seats that can be used by a person to sit on while another one lies on their back and engages in oral sex. It is almost as same as a smother box but comes with the option of being locked or restrained inside. Most of them will look like simple chairs while others can look like thrones.

Sofa chairs are also known as chaise lounges and are the next thing to wedges. They can support the entire body in order to promote different sexual positions. Some of them can come with restraints.

Thrones can be a type of bondage furniture. They can be altered to look like high back chairs and can be used in role-play.

Balls are more or less like exercise balls that are popular in gyms and aerobic classes. The ones used in the world of sex will have a dildo attached to them.

Bondage equipment can be of many types including crosses, benches, stocks etc. Remember that it is important to understand this equipment and not use them without knowing how. They come with their own set of pros and cons and you must know how to use them correctly.

Sex gliders refer to stools or straddles that can rock back and forth. The momentum generated can help to thrust or withdraw a dildo into the stool.

They are generally used for independent play and can leave your hands free to do whatever you wish to.

Sex swings and slings are popular sex furniture. Swings are unlike regular swings and the person sitting on them can derive pleasure. Some can be fixed to doorframes and some can cascade from the ceiling or remain independently. They help with thrusting and can be used to make difficult positions easier to get into.

Costs

Remember that none of the above-mentioned furniture will be cheap. Most of them will be custom pieces and can be quite expensive. Expect to pay anywhere from hundreds or dollars to a few thousands if you wish to set up a dungeon room. Even if you are buying from online stores such as Amazon, it can prove to be quite a costly affair. But it will be important to pay attention to the quality, manufacturing design and durability. These things are important to consider when you are looking for lasting pieces to buy. Inspect the pieces before buying them and make sure you do not get cheated.

Go for versatile pieces that can be used to serve different purposes. Before you buy any of the furniture, make sure there is adequate space to accommodate it.

If you are going for a customized piece then it might take some time, say a month or two and thus, you might have to wait a little before throwing your sex parties.

Materials

The list of materials that can be used to make this type of furniture can be endless. Right from foam to metal to wood to silicone to plastic to leather, there can be several materials that are necessary to make the equipment.

Here are some important things to keep in mind while choosing furniture for your sex dungeon.

- Can the furniture be cleaned easily?

- Is the furniture going to be porous?
- How many people might use it?
- How soft will the material be and will it be comfortable to use?
- How much wear and tear will be involved

If you are going for sex toys that have detachable parts then make sure they can be detached and stored for your convenience. It is ideal for rockers to be made of silicone so that they are easier to clean and maintain.

Consider adding restraints and other such features to your furniture to take them up a notch. Just attaching a few hooks can help you come up with interesting positions. But make sure the piece of furniture can take it and does not end up being unable to take heavy use that weakens its structure.

Storage

If you have only a limited space to work with then go for furniture that can be inflated or collapsed and is small enough to be tucked away into small spaces. You can also opt for furniture that is versatile and comes with storage options. For example, go for a sex bed with a cage or drawers attached to it so that you can store all the equipment inside.

When going for sex toys, make sure you look at the returns and warranties policies. You have to read the fine print to make sure you are going for the right furniture. Many aspects will require careful considerations including any moving parts of the machine, its motor, the fabrics used etc.

If there is any additional equipment that is being showcased or shown in the pictures then make sure you ask them if they will be supplied with the furniture or will be sold separately.

You must ensure that the seams are not sharp and check them out in person. Safety should be priority when using sex furniture. Speak with the seller beforehand and make sure you buy all the equipment that can be used safely.

Lubes-gels, oils, Nuru gel

Lube refers to a liquid that is used to make the vagina wet and that makes it easier to have intercourse. These are usually used to make the process smoother for women who suffer from dryness. It is convenient to use and can be used by just about anyone. But make sure you understand the pros and cons associated with it in order to use it correctly. They are explained as follows.

Lubes can be made of different materials including petroleum, silicone etc. One of the best types of lubes, however, happens to be water-based as these are less likely to cause irritation to your lady parts and can be safely used with condoms.

It is best to avoid petroleum-based lubes as they can end up breaking the condom. This can lead to unwanted pregnancies. So, avoid this as much as possible.

Lubes that contain glycerin can lead to yeast infections. They might be edible lubes that come is various flavors but would be best to avoid them.

Use lubes as a part of engaging in foreplay with your partner. Getting them to apply it on you can prove to be a fun and sexy activity. Be creative with it and use it as a way to make sexy time more fun with your partner.

Most lubes will be versatile and can be used by both men and women. They can also be used with sex toys to make it easier for them to glide.

Avoid using things you get in the kitchen such as oils and Vaseline as they might not be the right choice. They might end up causing irritation and infections. They might also damage the condom and lead to a break.

Nuru gels are quite popular and can be used during Nuru massage. These are known as full body massages and have become quite popular over the years. This is mostly owing to the easy availability of the Nuru massage gel or oil. It is very easy to use it and can end up being an extremely fun activity.

The word Nuru refers to slippery and is an intimate massage. The couple involved use the liquid to massage each other by taking turns to rub the oil down each other's bodies. This creates a slick surface over the skin. This leads to sensual foreplay. If you are interested in trying out Nuru massage then here is a simple guide.

Choosing the right surface

It will be important to choose the right surface to carry out the Nuru experience. If you are going for the true experience that can help you enjoy yourself then you will need a slippery surface to start with. Go for vinyl air mattress or Nuru specific massage sheets that can be made from water resistant plastic. You cannot use normal sheets for this as the liquids can soak through the sheets and mattress.

Lubricant

The next step is going for the right lubricant. Make sure you use a water-based lubricant to carry out the massage to have the best experience. It can be used to massage all parts of the body and will glide on smoothly. Most of these will be concentrated and you can add water to make it thinner. It is ideal to prepare the gel a few minutes before starting the massage so that the liquid can be spread easily all over the body. Most of the products will be inexpensive and safe for use by just about anyone. But try not to use them as lubes as that is not their intended purpose. Read the instructions on the pack carefully before using them to know how they can be safely used. Use a lube for your lady parts and Nuru gel for other parts of the body.

Shower together

Once you engage in the massaging session, shower with your partner. This is usually an important step involved in Nuru massaging. It helps in two ways viz, it gets rid of any dirt and other germs that might have travelled to the skin during the massage process and you will have an intimate experience with your partner in the shower. Secondly, extra water will enhance the slippery quality of the gel. So, do not wipe off the gel or dry yourself before taking a shower and go into the shower directly.

Massage and play

Make Nuru a fun activity for yourself and your partner. Take turn massaging each other and try our different techniques. Following an online video can make it easier for you to carry out the massage. You can focus on a specific part every time so that it can be a fun experience. Use slippery mattresses and pillows for a fun experience. Use a towel to dry your hands and ensure they are free of gels.

Once you are done, get back into the shower and use soap and water to take the gel off. Remember that the gel can make some surfaces very slippery so you have to exercise caution. If you have Nuru sheets and pillows then read the instructions to know how to clean them and dry them to be used next time.

Research the best lubes that can be used for the experience. Read the product's testimonials to ensure the gel is ideal for use and will suit you.

What are Sex Toys?

Sex toys are used to enhance sexual experience. In other words, they are used to make sex a more enjoyable and fun experience for both the man and the woman. There is no limit to what can be used as a sex toy and you can pretty much go for regular household things. But you must ensure that it is safe to use them and that it will not lead to injury or infection. It would be a good idea to stick with traditional sex toys such as vibrators and masturbators. There are countless sex toys available and you can go for whatever you think fits your bill.

Buying sex toys

Now that you know what sex toys are and have made up your mind about them, it is time to do some shopping. Here are some things that you must know about before you get down to buying the toys.

- It will be important to pay attention to the material that has been used to make the sex toy. The material will determine how you use the sex toy and how you care for it. If you are looking for a soft and flexible option then go for a toy made of silicone. If you are looking for something firmer then go for toys made of plastic or glass.
- It would be a good idea to make a budget for the toys. You will be able to buy some basic things such as penis rings and dildos cheaply. But if you are looking for something more exotic then consider getting a luxury vibrator. These are unique vibrators that can be operated using smartphones. They can be controlled from just about anywhere. This can make for a unique and interesting experience for you and your partner.
- Preplan the size of the toy. Before buying them, make sure you determine the size of the toy so that you can be comfortable while using it. Nobody wants to end up with a sex toy that is too

big or too small. So, make sure you analyze the various sizes available and go for the best fit.

Using sex toys

Once you finally buy the sex toys, it is time to learn to use it. Although it might seem like a straightforward task, you have to learn some of the procedures involved. Here are some tips.

- Before you start using your sex toy, make sure you give it a good wash. Next, look for a comfortable place where you can peacefully use the toy. You should focus on enjoying the toy and pleasure yourself to the fullest.

- Next, grab a bottle of lube and apply it over the sex toy and also yourself. As you know, if you are pleasuring by yourself then there will not be any foreplay and thus, you will have to use a lube to get things rolling. Women too will need lubes in order to do it the right way.

- It will be a good idea to start slowly when using a sex toy. Do not go all in at once as that might lead to injury. Ease yourself in and make sure the toy hits the pleasure points. Once you start getting comfortable with the toy, you can use it to your liking.

- If you are getting your partner to use it on you then guide them through it so that you can have a pleasurable experience.

Cleaning the toys and tips on maintenance

It is important to clean and care for your toys to make sure that they can be easily used the next time. Here are some tips to help you clean your toys every time you use them.

- Clean your toys before using them each time by spraying a little antibacterial on them. You can buy specific antibacterial that is meant to clean sex toys. Once done, wipe it off using a lint free towel. Read the instructions on the packaging to establish whether it is safe to use soap and water on the toy and that this will not lead to any damage.

- When using lubes with your sex toys, ensure that you go for water-based ones. They will be gentle on the toy and easy to use. Some lubes might contain chemicals that can react with certain materials such as rubber. You can also use condoms if you want to make the toy a little easier to use.
- Make sure you keep your sex toys away from each other. Some sex toys can end up reacting with each other and thus, it would be best to keep them separated. Try to store sex toys in their own storage boxes and bags for safekeeping.

Types of sex toys

Here are some types of sex types you can try out.

- Clitoral vibrators happen to be toys that are meant to stimulate the clitoris to attain sexual pleasure and orgasm. These vibrators will not be used to penetrate into the vagina and only to stimulate the clitoris. Knowing where you feel most pleasure can help you place the vibrator in the right spot. As you know, you might not be comfortable storing a vibrator in your room in case it is accidentally discovered, thus, vibrators that look like everyday objects are also available. They will not look like vibrators but as mere objects such as sponges, mobile phones etc.
- There are many types of vibrators available for clitoral stimulation and they can be designed to serve specific purposes. Some of them include the following.
- Hands free clitoral vibrators are meant to be used to stimulate the clitoris and the labia. These do not require the use of hands and can be strapped into place using belts so that the hands are free. Some examples of this type of vibrators include butterfly strap on and rings.

- Butterfly strap on toys happen to be made in the shape of butterflies, flowers or animals. They come with adjustable straps that can be harnessed around the waist or hips of women.
- Vibrating panties refer to panties that tend to vibrate when worn. They can induce a local vibration and can be controlled using a remote and worn under regular clothing.
- Cock rings are like vibrating bullets that are used to stimulate the clitoris during intercourse. The clitoral vibrator and erection enhancer are both used to stimulate the vagina for pleasure.
- One of the most common type of vibrators is the manual vibrator that comes in a host of designs. They are traditional vibrators and widely used. But they can be difficult to use as they have to be held in the hand and might not provide the same level of pleasure as some of the other vibrators. Some of them can be water proof in nature and that means they can be freely used in the shower.

Male sex toys

One of the most common types of male sex toys is the cock ring. They are to be added to a semi erect penis and go around the base of the shaft. This clamps down the arteries and can lead to a super erect penis. These are some of the oldest forms of male sex toys and still happen to be popular around the world.

Choose a cock ring made from a comfortable material such as silicone. Some use steel cock rings to enhance their erection. Soft plastic is also a good option to pick. Once you buy it, clean it using a cleaner before use.

Slip it on a semi-erect penis by gently pushing it on. Remember that the ring should not be too tight and should be comfortably worn around the shaft.

Fleshlight is another popular male sex toy that has been in use since the mid '90s. It comes in the shape of a flashlight with a vagina like opening at the tip. A man is simply supposed to insert his erect penis into the fleshlight to derive pleasure.

Sex dolls are also available in different shapes and sizes. These are basically life size dolls that come with breasts and pussies and can look realistic. These can actually make men feel like they are holding a real girl. But these can be quite expensive and range from tens of thousands of dollars depending on the model.

Pros and cons of using sex toys

Sex toys are quite common these days and are advertised to catch the attention of both grown-ups and teens. Women of any age can use these toys for pleasure and enhance their sexual pleasure. These toys can be used during foreplay to enhance sexual pleasure. Although most toys are safe to use and can provide sexual pleasure, there are some reasons that make women reject them. Here is a list of advantages and disadvantages of sex toys.

Pros

- There are a wide variety of sex toys available on the market and you can explore as many as you like. They can be used to enhance sexual pleasure and induce foreplay. They can be used to enhance your mood.
- It is not new that women love to explore their bodies and understand their erogenous zones. These sex toys can be used to serve this purpose. They can increase the pleasure felt during sex and increase sexual interest and pleasure. It can also enhance self-confidence and make women more confident in bed.
- They can be used to enhance orgasms by stimulating different pleasure points.

The toys can be adjusted for speed and timing to provide maximum pleasure.

- If women start using sex toys regularly then they might end up using them every time instead of having sex with their partners. It might end up giving more pleasure than sex.
- Some women might get too used to the toys and not be able to cum. They will need vibrations to cum and might not be able to do so during intercourse.
- It will be important to maintain clean toys to avoid infections and also maintain the quality of the toys.

Sex robots

Sex technology is on the rise with more and more sex toys making it onto the market. It is becoming a paradise for single men and women who seek to pleasure themselves artificially. Sex robots are still in developmental stages but there are a few that are already available for use. They are customizable dolls that can be used to seek pleasure without the hassle of a relationship. Here are a few pros and cons associated with such robots.

- These robots can help to prevent sexually transmitted diseases. People can freely use them to derive sexual pleasure without worrying about STDs. But care must be taken not to share them with others.
- Sex happens to be a very basic human need and is fulfilled by the robot. Being lonely or deprived of sex can negatively impact a person's mental wellbeing. Having regular sex can help to release stress and prevent depression. A sex robot can help to drive away some of the blues.

Cons

- If people start depending on robots for sex then they will begin to lose interest in having sex with their partners. There might come a time when human connect will be lost. People's definition of intimacy will change and they will begin to look at robots as their partners.

- Not having a partner might lead to stress. Losing contact with humans can make it tough to have a regular life.
- You might end up compromising on a normal relationship.

Reasons to use sex toys

Sex toys are popular around the world and one of the things people resort to when it comes to spicing up their sex life. Whether it is a vibrator or a cock ring that you are using, sex toys can help you spruce up your sex life.

What's more, it is perfect for people who are single and do not have a partner to have sex with. Once you start using sex toys, you will be amazed at the pleasure you can derive from them.

But sadly, not many people use sex toys or perhaps think of them as taboo or are ashamed to have them around for fear of being discovered. They do not realize what they are missing out on and the amount of pleasure they can derive from using the toys.

If you introduce it during sex with your partner then you can further enhance your experience and take your sex life to the next level. If you are still unsure about them and need a little nudge to start using sex toys then here are ten reasons that will make you change your mind about them.

Pressure off

As you know, it is not easy to orgasm despite your partner giving you their all. As per experts, around 70% women need some kind of clitoral stimulation to achieve an orgasm or climax. Although it is always an option to use the tongue or fingers to stimulate the clitoris, it might not be possible always and will depend on the position. In such a case, simply reaching out to a vibrator can help you massage and stimulate your clitoris. This can help to take the pressure off you and help you orgasm every time you have sex with your partner. You can teach your partner how to use the vibrator so that they can use it on you during sex.

Ease partner

Sex toys can put your partner at ease. Regardless of how hard your partner tries, they will not be able to stimulate the same way as you stimulate yourself. By bringing a sex toy to bed, you can achieve an orgasm and that will take pressure off your partner. Sex will turn into a relaxing activity and one that can help you feel relaxed and at peace every time you have sex.

Multiple orgasms

One of the advantages associated with using sex toys is that you can increase the number of orgasms that you have. You do not have to settle for just one every time you have sex. You can have multiple orgasms in one go. Not only can it help you enjoy sex more but also help your partner enjoy more. As per experts, using vibrators can greatly enhance sexual pleasure and satisfaction. You will be going for extreme pleasure and can keep up with a session for hours.

All about exploring

Exploring your body using toys can make it interesting for you and your partner. It can help you establish a greater sexual bond with your partner. The memories you create with your partner can last you forever. Say, you can never forget the first man who inserted a dildo into you. There are a whole host of toys that you can use which go beyond basic dildos. Some include the likes of remote-controlled stimulators that your partner can use to control from any part of the room or any part of the world. You can use interesting anal gems or butt plugs to play with the anus. There are also blindfolds and dildos that you can use or go for nipple clamps and gag balls. We will look at these toys in detail in the last chapter.

Try out new positions

Sex toys can encourage you to go for new positions. You might have heard that there are about 64 sex positions to try out. But by being a little creative you can have many more than that. Using sex toys can help you explore new positions and enhance your sex life. As mentioned, there are a variety of toys to choose from and you can go with whatever you think can help you increase your pleasure.

Company

The next time you are masturbating, you can have company. We all know that masturbating is good for the body but having a partner join in can make for an even better experience. It can also prove to be an educational experience, as you will know what pleases your partner in bed and what they would like you to do. Similarly, you too can show them what gives you pleasure and how you should be stimulated. Show them how you use the toys and the points where you feel most pleasure.

Fantasies

Your sex toys can help you enhance your fantasies. Right from engaging in role-play to using props to enact movie scenes, sex toys can be used to increase your sexual experiences. Spice it up by dressing up and using different props while having sex. Do not limit yourself to traditional ones such as handcuffs and whips and go for interesting ones such as app-controlled toys. You will never get bored with your toys as they can be used to enact a different situation each time.

Breaking taboo

There is some stigma associated with sex toys that make people believe it is only ideal for single women who wish to avoid partners to explore sex with. But this is false. Men do not have to feel intimidated by a woman using sex toys for pleasure. They can join them in using the toys to explore their sexuality. It can be fun for not just the one using the toy but also the one helping with the usage.

Gifts

Sex toys can make for amazing gifting options. You can surprise your partner with a new toy to spruce up your sex life. The toy does not have to be something that your partner can use on themselves but can also be things that can be used on you. Surprise them with things they have never used before.

Shopping together

Shopping for sex toys with your partner can help you bond better with them. There are a lot of toys out there to choose from and you can make it a fun experience by going sex toy shopping with them. There can be a variety of things to choose from and you can engage in a little trial and error to find the right toys to use in bed with your partner.

Sex toys in the shower

It is no secret that having sex in the shower can be a fruitful experience. But is it possible to take your favorite sex toy along? Let us find out.

Finding the right sex positions in the shower can prove to be a tough task especially if you have limited space and the tiling makes things slippery. In such a case, investing in some non-slip mats or handles to hold on to while in the shower can help you explore your sexual side in the shower. You can try out a whole host of positions and experiment with new ones knowing that you will be safe in the shower. Some of these won't even require you to drill holes and can be attached using suction cups.

Shower head

It is not secret that most women use showerheads to seek pleasure while in the shower. They use the stream of water to stimulate their clitoris and can also use it to jet water into the vagina. But did you know that this showerhead could also be used to pleasure him in the shower? All you have to do is adjust the temperature of the water to make it a little more pleasing to his skin and direct it to the underside of his penis, where he feels sensitive. Tis can stimulate him and lead to a bigger and better erection.

Female ejaculations

The shower happens to be the right place to get her to ejaculate. One factor that mostly holds women back from ejaculating on the bed is getting it wet. In such a case, stimulating them on the shower can help them ejaculate peacefully. This can be better done in the bathtub where you can stimulate her to ejaculate without worries. Stimulate her G-spot and get her to come.

Waterproof toys

Invest in waterproof toys that can be taken to the shower or under water. There will be a range of products including vibrators and dildos that will be comfortable for use in the shower and will not slip out of your hands. You can also go for regular items in the shower such as rubber duckies that can be used as sex toys.

Take a lubricant along

Do not forget to take a lubricant with you to the shower. Lubricants can be important when you wish to have a sexual experience in the shower. Water has the tendency of stripping away natural lubricants and thus, you might need help from some lubes. But make sure you pick a lubricant that goes with your sex toy. Silicone lubricants and silicone sex toys will not be a good match.

Bondage toys

BDSM has existed for a long time but not everybody will know about the toys that are used. If you are new to BDSM and would like to explore some of the toys and concepts involved then here are some things to keep in mind.

Before you get started with it, it will be important to have everything ready to be used. Right from the toys to the equipment, the whole room should be set up so that you can engage in BDSM activities with your partner. These can be regular things that are easily available at home or thing that you specifically bought from a BDSM store.

Here are ten things that can get you started with it.

Blindfold

When it comes to BDSM, one of the main features is sensory deprivation. If certain senses are removed then the others tend to become magnified. If you are blindfolded then your sense of hearing and smell will become quite enhanced. You will begin to smell and hear things better. You need not use a traditional blindfold and go for items that are lying around the house. Some include sleeping masks or scarves that can be used to blindfold your partner. Some might also be interested in using masks that can restrict vision to some extent but not fully. These can be comfortable and not intimidate the person being blindfolded. Masquerade masks make for a good choice too and can be used to make it sexy.

Gag

As mentioned, taking away some of the senses is a big part of BDSM. Just by taking away the ability to speak, you will be able to enhance the other senses such as smell and sight. Gagging refers to stuffing the mouth with an item so that speech is restricted. You can use anything to gag your partner such as a gag ball that you can buy from an online or BDSM store or a piece of cloth. You can also simply tie a scarf around their mouth. It can be quite sexy to stuff your panties in his mouth.

Restraints

Restraints are commonly used in BDSM scenes and there can be many options to choose from. There can be inexpensive ones and also some expensive ones. The former might be disposable ones that can be used once and disposed of while the latter can last you a long time. Going for soft restraints can make it comfortable for you and your partner. Soft Velcro based handcuffs or leg cuffs can make for good starting equipment. If you wish to engage in role-play then go for a clothesline that can be used to tie the person and will make a good replacement for bondage ropes. It is best to avoid using zip ties and handcuffs if you are new to BDSM. They can become uncomfortable and lead to pinches. It might be a good option to use cloth-based ties and avoid duct tapes as they can irritate skin.

Pinwheels

Consider using pinwheels on your lover's body as you can derive pleasure from it. These pinwheels look like small pizza cutters that have small spikes at the end. They are meant to be rolled on your lover's body but it will be important to be gentle with it as otherwise it can lead to piercings on the skin. Try it over your skin first to make sure that it is gentle enough to be used on someone. These are usually rolled over sensitive areas of the skin such as the area around the nipples or groin region etc. Some of them might even vibrate and lead to a pleasurable experience.

Body clamps

Body clamps refer to clamps that can go around a whole host of areas including the labia, penis, tongue, nipples or testicles. They happen to be tweezer like clamps that come with grips and can be placed around any of these areas. Most of them can come with light pressure clamps while some such as the Japanese clover clamps are designed for those who can tolerate high pressure. If you are just starting out with it and need something simple to begin with then go for wooden clothes pins that can be used around the nipples or the genitals. Make sure the person is comfortable and not in pain.

Dildos and vibrators

The most widely used toys in the world of BDSM are dildos and vibrators. Vibrators in the shape of wands arc used as massagers and a cordless version makes for a perfect tool to attach someone's body using a rope or bondage tape. These vibrators can be used to reach the pleasure points and arrive at consensual orgasms. Anal vibrators also exist. These are not designed for use in vulvas and penises alone and can also be used as butt plugs. Getting the ones specifically designed for BDSM activities can help you have a more pleasurable experience.

Riding crop

Riding crops refer to tools that can be used to deliver a mild sting based on how they are used. They can be used to smack over the genitals or nipples. Using a sturdy riding cropcan help to serve as a cane. But be gentle with it as it can be quite powerful and impactful and pack a powerful punch.

Cane

A cane is available in a whole host of materials including plastic and wood. But canes can be painful as they can be hard and sturdy. They are not ideal for people who cannot resist strong pain. Just a little force can deliver a painful mark on someone. So, it is best to be used on someone who is used to BDSM and can tolerate the pain. You need not turn to commercially available canes and can go for something in your house that can act as a makeshift cane. Ensure that you are gentle and do not hit the person with too much force.

Flogger

A flogger is like a cane but much softer and wider. It can be used to deliver less painful hits. Leather and faux-leather ones happen to be quite popular options. If you are looking to deliver a stinging feeling then choose heavier faux leather ones that can be thin and stiff. Floggers that are made using rubber or nylon can be extremely painful and have to be used with caution.

Paddle

A paddle can be wooden or plastic or metal or made from faux leather. Some might have a mixture of many materials that can make it heavy and ideal to bee used to derive various types of sensations. If you happen to be working with a budget then it would be best to go with things that are easily available in your house such as wooden spoons and spatulas or hairbrushes. If you wish to soften it then use a car-washing mitt over it.

Apart from these items, there are also some other ones such as medical gloves, condoms, lubes, safety scissors, baby wipes and towels that you will need while engaging in BDSM.

Always start with the basics and then move to the advanced options in BDSM. If you go for too much right from the beginning then it can end up becoming too overwhelming for you and your partner. Buy fancy equipment only after you get comfortable using the basic ones.

Remember to get creative with whatever you have available. Do not rely on props all the time to make it fun; you have to unleash your inner wild side to be able to enjoy the experience.

Chapter 18 -
Sex Dictionary

Anal beads

Anal beads refer to sex toys that consist of many spheres or balls that are all attached or held together using plastic or wood skewers and are inserted into the anus or rectum and then drawn out using varying speeds based on the desired effect. These anal beads help to stimulate the pleasure points inside the rectum and can lead to a pleasurable experience. This is ideal for use with those who are used to having anal penetrations and best to avoid for those who are new to it and have tighter sphincters.

Anal vibrator

An anal vibrator is a type of vibrator that is designed to produce sexual stimulation of the anus. They vibrate in order to produce a vibrating effect inside the anus that leads to a pleasurable experience.

Bread dildo

The Bread dildo is said to have been prepared using bread and is a legend from the Greco Roman era dating around 2,000 years ago. Some companies have tried out this concept in recent years but none have been successful in making it a popular fad.

Butt plug

Butt plugs refer to sex toys that are meant to enter the anus to derive sexual pleasure. They can resemble a dildo but will be shorter and stubbier. They will have a flanged end to them that are meant to keep them from getting lost inside the rectum.

Candy Girl

Candy girls refer to a line of realistic looking dolls that are made by a Japanese company known as orient industries. These dolls are known for their aesthetic appeal and look quite realistic. These dolls can vary in their pricing depending on how realistic they are and can go from $1,500 dollars to $7,000. They are not easily available and have to be bought from Japan through shopping deputies.

Cock ring

Cock rings are rings that are worn around the base of the penis. The main use of wearing these is to restrict the flow of blood from an erect penis to produce a stronger erection or maintain an erection for a longer period of time. Some might use these as an item to decorate their genitals. These rings are better known as penis rings, C rings or shaft rings and can be used by those who suffer from erectile dysfunction. Another type of cock ring is a cock crown or gland ring. There are tucked behind the corona of the penis. Rings that go around the scrotum or penis are known as cock ball rings. Cock rings that hold the testicles are referred to as ball stretchers.

Dildo

A dildo is a fairly common sex toy that looks like a dick or has a phallic appearance. It is meant to be inserted into the vagina to replace a regular cock. It can be used independently by women or used during sexual intercourse with a partner. Dildos can be made of a variety of materials including wood, plastic, rubber etc. They come in all sizes and thickness.

Double penetration dildo

A double penetration dildo is also known as a double dildo and refers to a sex toy that helps to penetrate two orifices at once. It is meant to be a double penetrative stimulator that can be fixed to a single shaft. Some might include a vibrating motor in order to deliver a better experience.

Erotic electro stimulation

Erotic electro stimulation refers to the act of using electrical stimulations that are delivered to nerves in the body, especially in the genital areas using tools such as violet wands and TENS that are meant to deliver low intensity shocks. These are mostly used in BDSM activities and meant to deliver intense sensations when placed over nipples or genitals.

Erotic furniture

Erotic furniture refers to sex furniture that can be used while engaging in the act of sex. This type of furniture is quite common at sex parties and clubs and is used to derive a better sexual experience. Some of the most common types of sex furniture include beds, couches, sofas etc. These can be specifically designed furniture that is meant to serve specific purpose. Some of them are described as under.

Sex Gliders

These refer to devices that use gravity to help people make love without the use of any complicated slings.

Fisting slings

These refer to angled foam wedges that are used to support women and get them into the right positions to aid in the act of fisting. They will be designed ergonomically to serve the purpose and will make it easier to carry out the specific activities.

Love bumpers

These refer to bondage equipment that include stocks and pillories.

Love chair

A love chair refers to a chair made using curved steel tubes and articulated at several angles that are meant to help in sexual acts that can be otherwise impossible to perform. This type of device was first introduced in a men's magazine during the mid '70s. It gained popularity at the time but is not easily available these days. Saw horses are shaped like tables that are used by carpenters but come with sharper edges and are meant to be sat upon to attain a feeling that is similar to crotch rope in bondage. The designs are said to have been inspired by the love bed that was made for King Edward VII who was overweight and used a special bed to make love to women.

Genital Jewellery

Genital jewelry is also known as sex or adult jewelry and is typically designed to be worn around the genitals to accentuate their appearance. There can be many types of genital jewelry such as rings and studs as also anal piercings. Nipple piercings are quite common and has thus received widespread acceptance. Some forms of genital piercings have existed since the Victorian era for example Prince Albert's piercings. It is said that people have used genital piercings to decorate their genitals for centuries. Some nudist beaches might not accept them as they can be considered to be overtly sexual in nature.

Love egg

A love egg is a sexual vibrator that is in the shape of an egg or a bullet and is used to stimulate organs. They are sometimes known as egg vibrators or bullet vibrators based on their shape. These vibrators can include small and discreet sex toys that are no more than two or three inches in length and about ¾ inches in width. Some of these will be less expensive and might not be as strong as some of the other vibrators.

Love chair

A love chair is a device made by a French manufacturer in the early 20th century for King Edward to have sex with two or more women at once.

Nipple clamp

A nipple clamp is nothing but a sex toy that is attached or applied to the nipples of people of all genders. It leads to a pain in the nipple area as blood flow is restricted and then reintroduced to the nipples. Nipple clamps are mostly used during BDSM activities such as during breast torture. One of the main types of clamps used in breast torture is the clover clamp or the piercing clamp and clothes pin style clamp. The two clamps will be connected using a chain that is usually hung from a high point in order to increase the level of pain that is felt. The chain can be wrapped around a piece of furniture such as a post and the post can be raised or pushed back in order to increase the sensation of pain. The person wearing it can be made to move suddenly in order to induce pain. Another version of this clamp involves attaching another chain to the main chain and the end of which are attached to the clitoris or a cock ring. These are better known as Y clamps owing to the shape of the chain and the points of the body where they are attached.

Orgasmatron

An Orgasmatron is a device that featured in the 1973 movie called sleeper and is said to have the same effects as an orgasmic orb. The same type of device has been featured in some other types of fictional works and also extend to some non-fictional devices that can be used to trigger of an orgasm like response by using electrodes at the base of the spine.

Sex dice

A sex dice is a type of dice-based game that is meant to enhance sexual gameplay. It is used to induce foreplay and involves the use of a dice that mentions a part of the body instead of numbers and the person rolls the dice and the body part that appears on top will invite sexual attention. This type of dice is usually used to break the ice and make sexual partners become more comfortable with each other. The dice can be used in the bedroom to enhance sexual activity and make it a little more interesting in the bedroom.

Sex doll

A sex doll is a life size doll that can be considered as a mannequin and is available worldwide as a doll that can be used to have sex with. It is a poseable doll with a PVC skeleton and silicone flesh. Some of these dolls can be lifelike with realistic expressions and realistic body parts.

Sex machine

A sex machine happens to be a fucking machine that can be used to stimulate the genitals and promote sexual activity. The device can be penetrative in nature or can also be extractive. A penetrative device works with the transfer of reciprocating force from the motor attached to a shaft that is tipped off by a dildo. A reciprocating saw like device is known as a fucksaw. And a hand-held drill motor rotating device is better known as a drilldo. A hand-held modified jigsaw is better known as a jillsaw. An extracting device can be attached to the breasts or the penis or any other such body part serves as a sex machine.

Sex pillow

A sex pillow is a special pillow that is designed specifically to serve as a utility tool to aid during sexual intercourse. You are free to use either an ordinary pillow or a specific one that is designed to assist with intercourse. Some of these pillows can contain a high- density urethane core that is meant to support and balance the woman and can also render softness. Apart from regular pillow shapes, they can also come in other shapes such as wedges, ramps, prism etc. This makes it easier to get into the different sexual positions. There are also medical pillows that are ideal for those who suffer from back pains and go below the woman's butt or hips during missionary position.

Sex swing

A sex swing is better known as a sling and happens to be a type of harness that is designed to incorporate sexual intercourse between people who are suspended by the swing and the other person can move freely. These swings can come in various sizes and shapes and can be used to support the stomach or the back or legs etc. These can be adjusted to suit the person's specific needs.

Sex toy industry in China

The sex or adult industry in China is extremely big and makes up 70% of the world's sex toys produced. It is estimated that the sex toy industry in China accounts for a whopping
$2 billion and has more than 1,000 manufacturers spread all around the country. As per reports, the revenue that is earned from this industry crosses over $950 million and incorporates some best-selling items that are meant to arouse sexually and stimulate

sexually.

Sex toy party

A sex toy party refers to a party for women where they gather to understand about sex toys and buy them. They are more or less compared to Tupperware parties. The host of the party will display and might even demonstrate the sex toys that are a part of the party. Although the parties can be quite explicit in nature, some euphemisms might be used to refer to the different body parts. The participants are allowed to use or discuss the products that are being displayed. Apart from toys, some other things such as salts and aromatherapy can be a part of these parties. The host or representative of such toys will be given a commission based on the number of sales. There are thousands of such representatives in the US as sex toy parties have existed since the 1970s and have led to alternative sexual practices.

Simulator Strap-on dildo

A strap on dildo is one that is designed to be worn around the hip or waist using a harness in order to promote sexual activity. These harnesses and dildos will be available in different styles to help wearers of all kinds to sport them and make it easier for them to use them. Strap on dildos can be used to serve a whole host of sexual activities such as oral sex, vaginal sex, mutual masturbation etc. Most of these will be used in combination with lubricants in order to make it easier to insert the dildos. They can be used by people of all genders and ages.

Tantus

Tantus refers to a company that makes silicone-based sex toys that include dildo, vibrators, butt plugs and strap on harnesses. They operate out of Nevada and happen to be one of the largest producers of silicone sex toys produced in the US. All of their products are made using medical grade silicone that can be considered to be quite safe and eco-friendly.

Virtual reality sex

Virtual reality sex is better known as VR sex and is a technological advancement that lets the users receive sensations from others who can be located in any part of the world. It is the same as computer-controlled sex toys that can promote such sensations. The users tend to wear virtual reality headsets so that they can see and interact with their partners.

Conclusion

In your sex life, you need to enter into a relationship with an open mind because every single person on earth has experiences that will shape the way that they respond in bed. A man who has performance issues will need a woman who helps him to boost his performance and feel good about himself. A woman who has issues about how good she is at sex will need helping along the way too. Bear in mind, it's not about you. It's about their past experience and what shaped their views on sex.

One couple that came for help were a couple that had waited until marriage because she had decided that she wanted to be pure when she married. He loved her and had sexual experience but since they had been together, neither one of them had approached the subject of sex. What they found was that they were so accustomed to a non-sexual relationship that they found it hard to make the transition. Her expectations of him were what held him back because he didn't know if he could live up to them. His expectations of her were what held her back as she knew he had slept with others and thought that he would compare.

Having visited a specialist in sexual matters, they decided to take the whole experience slowly, to discuss and to explore each other and to start to understand that sex between them was a new experience. There was no comparison to be made and she certainly should have no expectations, but should take one step at a time, discovering each other. Because both had that passion for each other, they went along with the advice and they even bought magazines and porn videos to help relax them into a situation where nakedness was natural between them and they were able to overcome all the difficulties together.

It doesn't matter what caused difficulties. Dialog and love can help you to overcome them. The problem that mankind has is that sex isn't something that you talk about openly in public and that makes it harder for couples to understand how to broach the subject in bed. Think of the bedroom as being a totally different arena where you can drop all of your inhibitions and discuss everything and when you do, you open up avenues for finding out what makes each other tick. Passionate kisses, learning about each other's bodies and enjoying your time together is vital to the sexual experience. Feel the passion and don't be afraid of it, but always respect your partner.

In this book we have covered all kinds of topics that should help you with your love life. The male point of view is different from the female point of view although the variations exist because sometimes women are more dominant or men are not afraid of their feminine side. Whatever your situation, you have to gage how to approach sex to suit your partner's mentality and to open up your understanding of each other. If you don't know how to react to something, step back from it and think about it, but don't leave it as a doubt in your mind. For example, if you are afraid of oral sex, tell your partner and he will be gentler with you. If you think that your male partner is too violent, slow him down and let him know you need a certain amount of gentleness. Never sleep on an argument but don't think that making up has to involve sex. It does sometimes and this can come as a bonus, but before you can get to a stage where that's what both of you want, you need to be open with each other.

Communicate with one another about what the other one likes and dislikes. Tell each other about your fantasies and what it takes to drive them crazy. Touch one another and tell each other how attracted you are to them, boosting each other's self-esteem can have amazingly positive effects on your sex life. One of the most important things you can do in a relationship is communicate with one another. Without communicating, you can't expect to learn anything about each other.

Enjoy your nakedness together. Explore each other's bodies and find out all of those sensitive areas. Be aware of what your partner sees as a turn-off as well and comparing notes in the early days of your relationship will help you to clear up any misconceptions you may have that may stunt your love life. The best way forward is to respect each other and never to criticize the way that making love happens. Simply let it evolve and if it doesn't, give it a little help. Between the two of you, you have the opportunity to make the passion continue, and that's what great lovemaking is all about.

Sexual relations are an important part of any human's life and without them, we may feel like less than human. That said, especially in this day and age, it is important to be very careful with whom and how you have sex. In a time when STDs are on the rise and unwanted pregnancies are a real problem, you will want to practice safe sex above all else. Don't just jump into bed with anyone and even when you do remember to use protection to keep yourself and your partner safe from the countless threats that are lurking.

For More From 24K Industries Click To Subscribe.

References

https://www.thrillist.com/sex-dating/nation/11-things-you-need-to-know-before- going-to-a-swingers-club#

https://www.cosmopolitan.com/uk/love-sex/sex/news/a44800/what-its-like-take- part-sex-orgy/

https://www.kinkly.com/definition/912/female-cuckold-bdsm
https://www.kinkly.com/definition/10202/cuckcake
https://www.literotica.com/s/dom-sub-swingers-party
https://www.bustle.com/articles/185252-how-to-explore-cuckolding-humiliation- fetishes

https://www.rewriting-the-rules.com/sex/dominant-and-submissive-relationships/

https://www.bustle.com/articles/183480-13-sexy-domination-submission-games-to- play

https://rekink.com/dominance-101/keep-your-sub-crawling-back-dominance-201/

https://onehallyu.com/topic/35025-the-queen-of-spades-subculture-sexual-freedom- or-slavish-stereotype-of-women/

https://www.quora.com/What-is-the-meaning-behind-a-Queen-of-Spades-tattoo https://www.lovense.com/sex-furniture https://101.lubezilla.com/featured-stories/introduction-to-nuru-massage/ http://www.gurl.com/2012/07/26/what-is-lube/ https://www.adameve.com/sex-guides/products/sex-toys/beginner-guides/sex-toys- guide-65770-1845.aspx

http://www.female-sex-toys.com/pros-cons-female-sex-toys/
https://en.wikipedia.org/wiki/Clitoral_vibrator
https://www.securesingle.com/3-pros-cons-singles-sex-tech/
http://malesextoy.net.au/types-of-male-sex-toys.html
https://en.wikipedia.org/wiki/Category:Sex_toys

https://www.lovehoney.co.uk/sex-toys/sex-toys-for-couples/buyers-guide/how-to- have-sex-in-the-shower/

https://www.kinkly.com/2/9692/sex-toys/the-top-10-bdsm-toys-for-beginners

https://www.bustle.com/articles/61586-10-hot-reasons-to-use-sex-toys-with-your- partner-in-bed